SUPER SCIENCE
ENCYCLOPEDIA

SMITHSONIAN

SUPER SCIENCE ENCYCLOPEDIA

AUTHORS JACK CHALLONER, DR. KAT DAY,
HILARY LAMB, GEORGIA MILLS, BEA PERKS
CONSULTANT JACK CHALLONER

CONTENTS

DK LONDON
Senior Art Editor Sheila Collins
Editor Vicky Richards
US Editor Kayla Dugger
US Executive Editor Lori Cates Hand
Picture Researcher Nic Dean
Illustrators Brendan McCaffery,
Adam Benton, Peter Bull, Gus Scott
Managing Editor Francesca Baines
Managing Art Editor Philip Letsu
Senior Production Editor Andy Hilliard
Production Controller Sian Cheung
Jacket Designer Surabhi Wadhwa-Gandhi
Jacket Design Development Manager
Sophia MTT
Publisher Andrew Macintyre
Associate Publishing Director Liz Wheeler
Art Director Karen Self
Publishing Director Jonathan Metcalf

DK DELHI
Senior Editor Virien Chopra
Project Art Editor Baibhav Parida
Project Editor Kathakali Banerjee
Art Editor Sifat Fatima
Picture Researcher Nishwan Rasool
Picture Research Manager Taiyaba Khatoon
Managing Editor Kingshuk Ghoshal
Managing Art Editor Govind Mittal
Senior DTP Designer Neeraj Bhatia
DTP Designer Anita Yadav
Pre-Production Manager Balwant Singh
Production Manager Pankaj Sharma

First American Edition, 2021
Published in the United States by DK Publishing
1450 Broadway, Suite 801, New York, NY 10018

Copyright © 2021 Dorling Kindersley Limited
DK, a Division of Penguin Random House LLC
21 22 23 24 25 10 9 8 7 6 5 4 3 2 1
001–310498–Aug/2021

A catalog record for this book is available
from the Library of Congress.
ISBN 978-0-7440-2890-4

DK books are available at special discounts
when purchased in bulk for sales promotions,
premiums, fund-raising, or educational use.
For details, contact: DK Publishing Special Markets,
1450 Broadway, Suite 801, New York, NY 10018
SpecialSales@dk.com

Printed and bound in China

For the curious
www.dk.com

MIX
Paper from
responsible sources
FSC® C018179

Established in 1846, the
Smithsonian is the world's
largest museum and research
complex, dedicated to public
education, national service, and
scholarship in the arts, sciences,
and history. It includes 19
museums and galleries and the
National Zoological Park. The
total number of artifacts, works
of art, and specimens in the
Smithsonian's collection is
estimated at 155.5 million.

This book was made with
Forest Stewardship Council™
certified paper—one small
step in DK's commitment to
a sustainable future. For
more information go to
www.dk.com/our-green-pledge

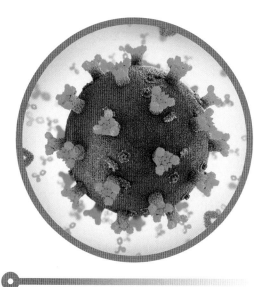

PROTECTING AND SURVIVING 120

LEARNING AND DISCOVERING 158

SCIENCE IN OUR EVERYDAY LIVES

Science is a way of finding out about the world around us. Scientists ask questions about what the world is made of and how it works and study the three main areas of science: physics, chemistry, and biology. But science isn't just theory—science is behind many things we rely on in the modern world, such as the light in our homes, the food we eat, and the clothes we wear. This book shows some of the ways scientific knowledge is put to use to help make our lives easier and find solutions to our problems.

PHYSICS

Physics is the study of energy and forces. Understanding physics allows us to design ways to get around, such as by bike or plane. The way our data travels over the internet also relies on knowledge of light gained by physicists.

BIOLOGY

Biology looks at how animals, plants, and other living things work. Learning about the human body allows scientists to develop crucial medicine, and understanding how trees grow can help us fight climate change.

THE SCIENTIFIC METHOD

There are many different areas of science, but most scientists follow a method in their quest to understand the world. The most important part of the scientific method is experimentation, which allows scientists to test their hypotheses (suggested explanations).

Observation

The scientific method begins with careful observation of some aspect of the world, something no one can yet fully explain. Scientists may observe something in a laboratory or in the wider world around us.

Hypothesis

Next, a scientist comes up with a possible explanation for their observation: a hypothesis. The hypothesis should be based on existing scientific knowledge and must be something that can be tested by carrying out an experiment.

Experiment

A scientist must design their experiments carefully, making sure they control as many aspects of the setup as possible. Typically, they will predict an outcome of the experiment that, if true, will support or disprove their hypothesis.

Analysis and theory

If a hypothesis is supported by the outcome of the experiments, that hypothesis may become part of a theory—a generally accepted part of science that may explain lots of different observations. Well-tested theories include the theory of evolution and the Big Bang theory.

CHEMISTRY

Chemistry is the study of how different substances react together. Using their knowledge, chemists can create new materials, such as synthetic textiles, and can also develop ways to extract key resources, such as salt.

FIELDS OF SCIENCE

Modern scientists are all specialists who work in one of many different fields. Some fall under the main subjects of biology, chemistry, and physics, while others combine knowledge from across these areas. A scientific breakthrough in one field can impact another—such as how the discovery of gene editing (how scientists can change the genes of living things) is now leading to advances in medicine and agriculture.

As science advances, new fields emerge, such as **synthetic biology** (building artificial living things).

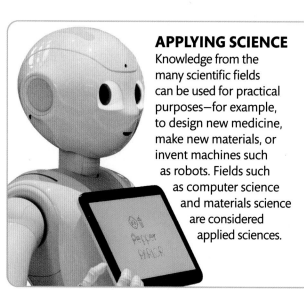

APPLYING SCIENCE
Knowledge from the many scientific fields can be used for practical purposes—for example, to design new medicine, make new materials, or invent machines such as robots. Fields such as computer science and materials science are considered applied sciences.

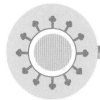

BIOCHEMISTRY
Biochemists study the complicated chemical reactions that take place inside cells and keep living things alive.

GENETICS
Geneticists work out how DNA (deoxyribonucleic acid) carries information within cells and passes it on to new generations.

FORENSIC SCIENCE
Forensic scientists use biology, chemistry, and physics to analyze evidence gathered at crime scenes in order to help investigations.

GEOLOGY
Geologists study the rocks and minerals our planet is made of and the enormous forces that shape the landscape.

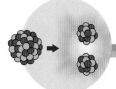

NUCLEAR CHEMISTRY
Nuclear chemists study the nuclei (the central part) of atoms and how different nuclei break apart.

BIOLOGY

Biology is the science of living things, from the structure of cells to how different organisms grow, behave, and interact with their environments.

CHEMISTRY

Chemistry is the study of substances such as elements, mixtures, and even tiny atoms. It looks at their properties and how they react together.

PHYSICS

Physics is the study of energy, force, and matter—the building blocks of everything, including sound, electricity, heat, magnetism, light, and the structure of atoms.

Zoology

Zoologists study the body structure and behavior of animals, as well as their evolution (how they developed over millions of years).

Microbiology

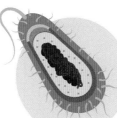

Microbiologists study organisms that are too small too see without a microscope—including bacteria and fungi.

Medicine

Medical scientists apply knowledge from many areas of biology, mostly human biology, to help cure disease and keep people healthy.

Botany

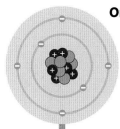

Botanists study the life cycles and structure of different plants and their evolution over time.

Ecology

Ecologists study the relationships between different species and between species and the places they live (habitats).

Paleontology

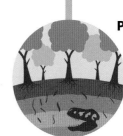

Paleontologists study living things that existed long ago, mostly through examining the fossilized remains of dead plants and animals.

Organic Chemistry

Organic chemists study reactions where the element carbon makes up one or more of the substances involved.

Electrochemistry

Electrochemists study how electricity is involved in reactions—how it can make reactions happen, or be produced by them.

Inorganic chemistry

Inorganic chemists study reactions that involve substances that do not contain the element carbon, most often those containing metals.

Particle physics

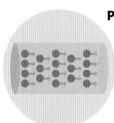

Particle physicists study the tiny particles smaller than atoms and how they interact with one another.

Mechanics

The study of mechanics is the study of forces and motion. Mechanics helps scientists understand machines.

Waves and vibrations

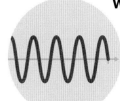

The study of vibrating objects and of sound, light, and other forms of energy that travel as waves.

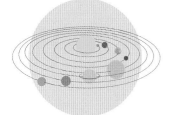

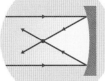

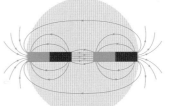

Astronomy

Astronomers study objects in space, including planets and moons, the Sun and other stars, and galaxies.

Thermodynamics

This area of physics is the study of how energy is transferred between objects as heat.

Optics

The study of how light interacts with various materials—in particula how it reflects o

Electromagnetism

Electromagnetism studies the i c ection

Meteorology

Meteorologists study the way heat interacts with air and water to produce different types of weather.

LIVING AND WORKING

There is science all around us in our daily lives. Using scientific techniques and methods, we can grow more food and conserve and clean the water we drink. The modern world is also kept running by the many different ways of harnessing energy scientists have developed, from wind turbines to nuclear reactors.

INDOOR FARMING
HYDROPONICS

While growing plants without soil or sunlight might seem strange, many large farms do this using a method known as hydroponics. In these indoor environments, the roots of plant seedlings are kept in a solution containing water and nutrients, and special lamps provide heat and light. Hydroponic farms can be constructed anywhere and operate all year round. The most common hydroponic crops are salad vegetables, such as lettuce and tomatoes, and soft fruits.

AQUAPONICS

Aquaponics combines hydroponics with aquaculture (fish farming). Plants are grown in a tank that is home to fish, crustaceans, or mollusks. These animals expel a substance called ammonia in their waste, which is harmful to them but an important nutrient for plants. The plants absorb the ammonia, keeping the water clean.

Plants grown using hydroponics need up to **90 percent** less water than plants in regular farms.

PLANT LIFE CYCLES

The life cycle of a plant such as a tomato plant begins when its seed is planted. The seed germinates into a seedling, which grows into a plant.

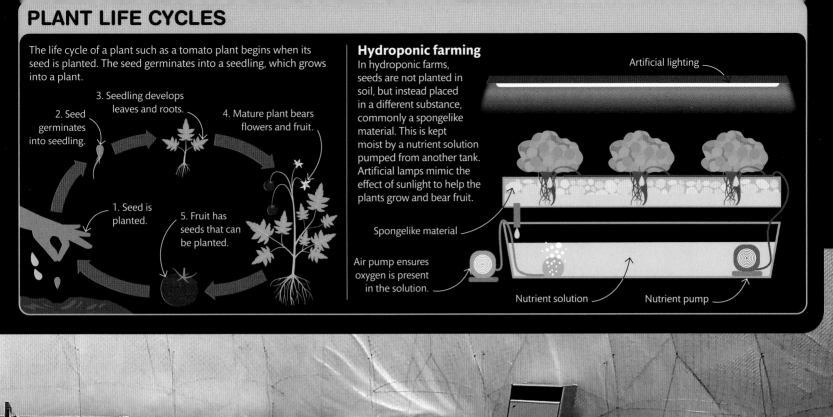

2. Seed germinates into seedling.

3. Seedling develops leaves and roots.

4. Mature plant bears flowers and fruit.

1. Seed is planted.

5. Fruit has seeds that can be planted.

Hydroponic farming

In hydroponic farms, seeds are not planted in soil, but instead placed in a different substance, commonly a spongelike material. This is kept moist by a nutrient solution pumped from another tank. Artificial lamps mimic the effect of sunlight to help the plants grow and bear fruit.

Artificial lighting

Spongelike material

Air pump ensures oxygen is present in the solution.

Nutrient solution

Nutrient pump

Lots of lettuce

At a hydroponic farm in Rikuzentakata, Japan, lettuce are planted in a circular bed. The bed rotates slowly and the seedlings move in a spiral toward the edge, growing over a period of 30 days. By the time they reach the edge, they are ready to be harvested.

SELF-LEARNING MACHINES

AUTONOMOUS ROBOTS

Many modern robots are autonomous, which means they can make decisions on their own. Robots that move and interact with their environment, such as self-driving cars or fruit-farming robots, use artificial intelligence (AI) to aid them. AI helps machines learn and enables them to make predictions or decisions based on information they already have, and therefore perform tasks with very little human supervision.

BURGER BOT

Robots are good at repetitive tasks, such as fast-food preparation. A robot called Flippy uses sensors to monitor burgers and other food items as they cook. It can tell when they need to be flipped and when they are fully cooked.

ARTIFICIAL INTELLIGENCE

A robot is said to have artificial intelligence when it can mimic how humans learn and make decisions. One way robots do this is by a technique called machine learning. They collect data (such as images), which they analyze to draw conclusions. When a farming robot takes a new image of a fruit, it is able to use what it has learned to identify the fruit and take action. The more images it takes, the more data it will have and the more its accuracy will increase.

1. The robot takes an image of a strawberry.

2. The AI recognizes features in the image.

3. The robot identifies the object and takes an action based on its conclusion.

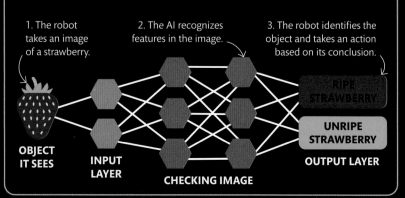

OBJECT IT SEES

INPUT LAYER

CHECKING IMAGE

RIPE STRAWBERRY

UNRIPE STRAWBERRY

OUTPUT LAYER

An autonomous fruit-picking robot can **pick** up to **794 lb** (360 kg) of strawberries in a day.

Fruit picker

Using AI, an autonomous robot such as the one shown here can tell if a strawberry is ripe and ready to be picked. It can then carefully pick the ripe berries with its gripper arm without bruising the soft fruit.

Treating soil

A farmer applies agricultural lime, which is made from finely ground limestone, onto the soil on a farm in Merseyside, UK. This raises the pH of the too-acidic soil so that it is closer to a neutral pH of 7, helping crops grow better.

IMPROVING THE SOIL
NEUTRALIZING ACIDS

Not all soil is the same—in some areas, it is more acidic than others. The chemical opposite to an acid is an alkali, and when these are added together, they neutralize each other. Because most plants grow best in soil that is neither too acidic or alkaline, sometimes farmers and gardeners add something alkaline, such as lime, to acidic soil. Mixing in lime not only neutralizes the soil, it also helps plants absorb nutrients. Worms and certain microorganisms needed for good soil also dislike acidic conditions, so it encourages them.

KRM Bredal

PLANTS AND PH

All plants are affected by the pH of the soil in which they are growing, and sometimes this can produce interesting effects. Hydrangeas like this one have blue flowers if they are growing in acidic soil but have pink flowers when grown in more alkaline soil.

ACIDS AND ALKALIS

Scientists describe how acidic or alkaline something is using the pH scale. On this scale, 0 is very acidic, 14 is very alkaline, and 7 is neutral. To test how acidic a substance is, scientists use indicators—substances that change color at different pH values. One of the best known is universal indicator, shown here. This is a mixture of indicators and turns different colors at different pHs.

ALKALINE						NEUTRAL							ACIDIC	
14	13	12	11	10	9	8	7	6	5	4	3	2	1	0

THE PH SCALE

Household bleach, along with some other cleaning products, is alkaline and has a very high pH.

The pH of pure water is 7, making it completely neutral.

Acidic foods such as vinegar and lemon juice have a low pH.

From grape to wine

The process of fermentation turns grape juice into wine. Yeast, a type of fungi, eats the sugars in the grapes and converts them to carbon dioxide and alcohol. The wine is then left to develop its flavor and color—here in oak barrels—which give it extra character.

Chocolate beans

Chocolate is made from the beans inside cacao pods. The beans are fermented under banana leaves for several days as fungi and bacteria develop flavours in them. They are then laid out in the Sun (above) until dry and ready for processing into chocolate.

Making bread

Yeast is the rising agent in bread making. This tiny fungus consumes the sugar inside the dough and releases carbon dioxide. Bubbles of this gas are trapped inside the dough and expand when it is cooked, causing the bread to rise and giving it a light, fluffy texture.

Researchers estimate that humans have been making cheese for 7,500 years.

ACTIVE INGREDIENTS

MICROBES IN FOOD

Microorganisms are tiny life forms not visible to the naked eye, and sometimes called microbes. While some have a bad reputation for causing disease, many of our favorite foods owe their flavor and texture to microorganisms. Microbes such as bacteria, yeast, or mold can change the chemistry of food in a natural process called fermentation. People have fermented food for thousands of years to make it last longer, taste better, or provide more nutrition

ADDING BACTERIA

In an early stage of the cheese-making process, cheese makers mix a yellow powder containing bacteria into vats of milk. Bacteria eat the energy-rich sugar inside milk and convert it into substances that allow the milk to harden.

FERMENTATION

Fermentation is a natural chemical reaction that happens when microbes consume food. Different kinds of microbes cause different types of fermentation. The creatures consume sugars inside the food—milk, in the case of cheese—and then convert them into substances that add flavor. In cheese, microbes eat the sugars and produce lactic acid, which not only flavors the cheese but also helps it last longer.

Microbes in a food consume its sugars.

Chemicals that add flavor are released as the sugar is consumed.

Sugars in the food

Carbon dioxide gas can be produced.

PROCESS OF FERMENTATION

Aging cheese

At a cheese aging cellar in France, a cheese maker taps the wheels of cheese to check how ripe they are. Some types of strong-tasting cheese are left to ripen for several years. This allows bacteria and mold to continue fermenting the cheese so that its rich flavors

Adding nutrients
Scientists from the John Innes Centre, UK,
have created genetically modified purple
tomatoes by adding a new gene from the
snapdragon flower to a regular tomato. This
increased the anthocyanin in the tomatoes,
a chemical thought to have a wide range
of health benefits and which could even
reduce the likelihood of getting certain
diseases, such as cancer.

CREATING NEW CROPS

GM FOODS

As the world's population grows, scientists are seeking to make food production more efficient. One way they can do this is through changing the properties of a food-bearing plant by altering tiny sets of instructions in its cells, called genes. The resulting genetically modified (GM) crops can be made to contain more nutrients, resist pests, or need less water to grow. They are carefully tested to ensure they are safe, but many people have concerns about the long-term effects of changing these crops.

NEW FRUITS

In the 1990s, the papaya ringspot virus wiped out papaya plantations in Hawaii. A variety of GM papaya, called rainbow papaya, was developed to be resistant to the virus and help the plantations thrive once again.

GENES

Genes are sections of DNA (see page 190), a substance found inside the cells of living things. They determine the characteristics, or traits, of living organisms. Genes are hereditary—an organism's offspring will inherit its genes from its parent or parents. In recent years, new technologies have been developed that allow scientists to modify the genes of plants and even animals.

Scientists are developing GM plants that can **survive in space** and feed **astronauts.**

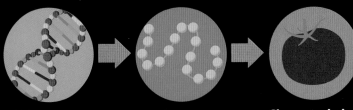

DNA
DNA is shaped like a double helix, which looks like a twisted ladder. Sections of it form genes.

Proteins
Each gene in a person's DNA is a code that tells cells to make different proteins.

Characteristic
Different proteins help make different characteristics in the organism, such as the color of a fruit.

EXPERIMENTS IN SPACE

GROWING PLANTS IN LOW GRAVITY

On the International Space Station (ISS), astronauts carry out many different experiments in a lab that's out of this world! These include examining how fire behaves in low gravity, studying radiation from stars, and growing plants in space. Plants not only supply fresh food, but are also great for the mental well-being of the astronauts. However, low gravity can affect the growth of plants. If astronauts used soil, this would float away, so instead they keep the plants' roots in protective pouches filled with nutrients.

EDIBLE GREENS

While much of the food on the ISS comes in pouches from Earth, fresh vegetables have begun to be grown on board. Future space exploration may take humans to farther-off places such as Mars, so it will be essential for astronauts to grow their own food.

PLANT GROWTH

To grow in space, plants need the same things as on Earth. The most important of these are water, minerals, and light. On the ISS, light comes from lamps. The heat from these lamps provides the right temperature for growth. Nutrients that are usually found in the soil are added to the water.

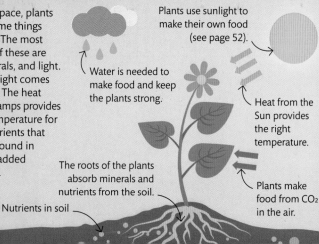

Plants use sunlight to make their own food (see page 52).

Water is needed to make food and keep the plants strong.

Heat from the Sun provides the right temperature.

The roots of the plants absorb minerals and nutrients from the soil.

Plants make food from CO_2 in the air.

Nutrients in soil

In 2015, astronauts ate a **space salad** with **freshly** harvested lettuce.

FROZEN FOUNTAIN
ICE STUPAS

Parts of the cold, dry, mountainous Himalayan region of Asia
receive only 2–2.7 in (50-70 mm) of rainfall in a year and experience
temperatures as low as –22°F (–30°C). While snow remains on the peaks
all year round, the lower regions are arid in the summer. Scientists have
developed a new way of freezing meltwater into mounds called stupas.
In this frozen state, water can be stored at high altitudes for irrigating
crops in the nearby fields.

Water store

This towering stupa was built by a group of young
engineers in the Leh district of Ladakh, India. It
serves as a water reserve. The cone shape means
the mass of ice has a relatively small area exposed
to direct sunlight. Because of this, it melts more
slowly than it would if it was in a flat layer. Because
it is hollow, a café has been opened inside.

SUMMER IRRIGATION

Farms in the Himalayan foothills rely on the
water that flows down from glaciers to survive,
but climate change is making the water supply
increasingly erratic. As Earth gets warmer,
glaciers are disappearing permanently, and
farmers have had to develop new ways of
storing water to irrigate crops in the summer.

Water spraying from the top freezes into ice in the cold air.

STATES OF MATTER

There are three states that all matter can exist in: solid, liquid, and gas. The ice in a stupa is a solid, but the same substance can also be water (a liquid) and vapor (gas). Solids have a fixed shape, because their molecules are held close together by strong bonds. Liquids and gases have weaker bonds, meaning liquids can change shape easily and gases have almost no shape. Ice stupas rely on the fact that liquid water can freeze into solid ice at a low temperature and ice can melt back into water at a higher temperature.

Solid
The molecules in ice are tightly packed together.

Liquid
The molecules in water have room to move.

Gas
The molecules in water vapor move freely.

Making an ice stupa

Engineers lay pipes up the mountain to collect water from glaciers. The flowing water is then fed up a tube and sprayed into the freezing air, causing it to turn into solid ice. As the temperature rises, the stupa melts.

Melting water from a glacier flows down a pipe.

Water is sprayed out.

Water freezes into ice, forming a stupa.

In the summer, meltwater flows down to fields.

ICE CAFE

A 70-ft (21-m) tall ice stupa can hold **500,000 gallons (1.9 million liters)** of water.

Fog catchers must face the direction of the wind.

HARVESTING WATER
FOG CATCHERS

In regions of the world with low rainfall, water can sometimes be collected from unusual sources. Fog catchers are simple structures that can catch the water droplets in fog, acquiring drinkable water without using any energy. They are a low-cost solution for areas with plenty of fog but little rain. Fog is made of countless tiny water droplets suspended in air. As wind blows fog through the mesh of the fog catchers, the mesh traps the water droplets.

MESH DESIGN
A fog catcher's net is not solid, because otherwise the wind would go around the catcher rather than through it. It is instead made of a fine mesh, which gives the net a large surface area so it can harvest as much water as possible from the fog.

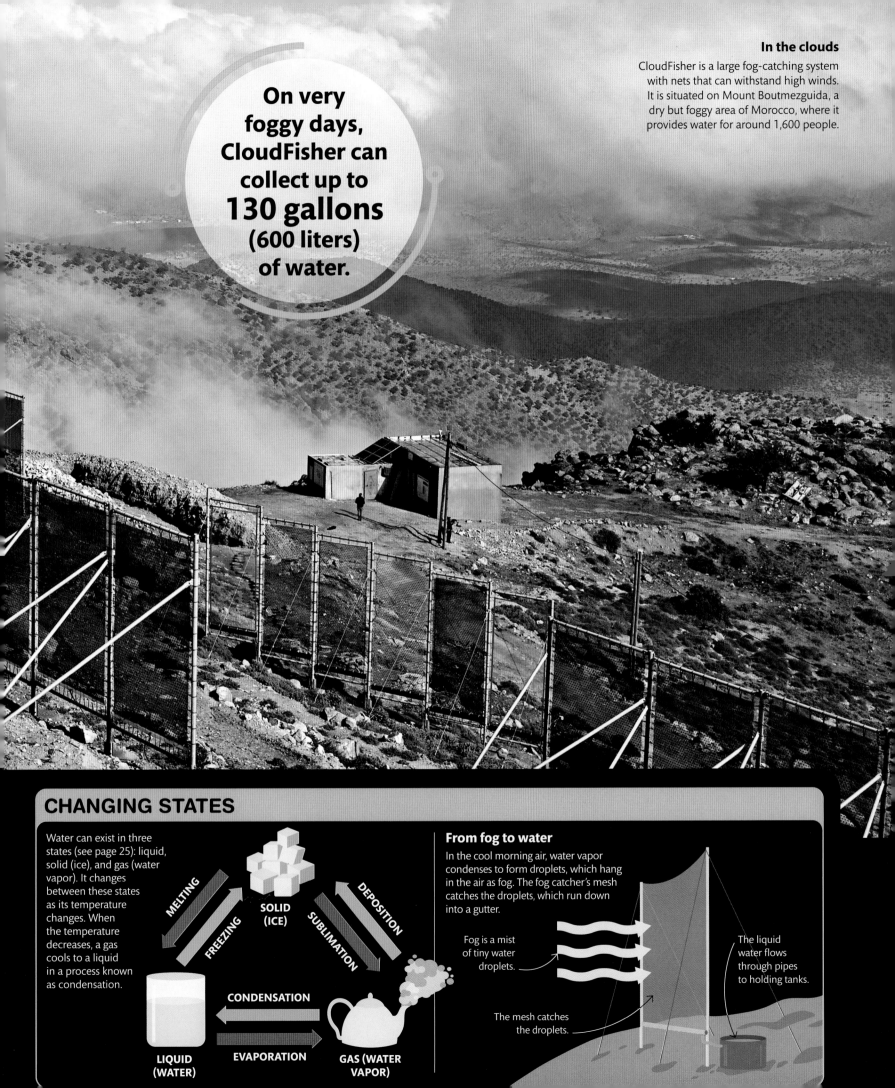

On very foggy days, CloudFisher can collect up to **130 gallons** (600 liters) of water.

In the clouds
CloudFisher is a large fog-catching system with nets that can withstand high winds. It is situated on Mount Boutmezguida, a dry but foggy area of Morocco, where it provides water for around 1,600 people.

CHANGING STATES

Water can exist in three states (see page 25): liquid, solid (ice), and gas (water vapor). It changes between these states as its temperature changes. When the temperature decreases, a gas cools to a liquid in a process known as condensation.

MELTING
FREEZING
SOLID (ICE)
SUBLIMATION
DEPOSITION
CONDENSATION
EVAPORATION
LIQUID (WATER)
GAS (WATER VAPOR)

From fog to water
In the cool morning air, water vapor condenses to form droplets, which hang in the air as fog. The fog catcher's mesh catches the droplets, which run down into a gutter.

Fog is a mist of tiny water droplets.

The mesh catches the droplets.

The liquid water flows through pipes to holding tanks.

EXTRACTING SALT

SEPARATING MIXTURES

The substance we call table salt has many uses, not just flavoring foods. It is mostly made of a mineral called sodium chloride, widely found on Earth but often dissolved in water. This cannot be filtered out, but it can be separated by evaporation. Where salty water is trapped in shallow pools, the heat of the Sun causes the water to evaporate, leaving behind piles of white salt.

Salt flats

Salt can be naturally extracted from large, flat areas of land called salt flats. The world's largest salt flat is Salar de Uyuni in Bolivia, an ancient lake that covers more than 3,900 sq miles (10,000 sq km). Salar de Uyuni is also a source of lithium, magnesium, and potassium.

WINTER ROADS

Salt is spread on roads in winter, where it mixes with rain and snow to form salty water. This has a lower melting point than pure water, so it stays liquid at colder temperatures. The roads are kept free of ice, making them less slippery and safer for drivers.

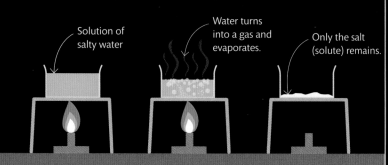

EVAPORATION

Salty water is a solution—a mixture in which one substance (the solute) is dissolved in another (the solvent). The salt is known as the solute. We can separate the solute from the solution by evaporation. The liquid water turns into a gas (water vapor), leaving solid salt particles behind.

Solution of salty water

Water turns into a gas and evaporates.

Only the salt (solute) remains.

1. The salty water is heated gently.

2. As the water evaporates, the solution becomes more concentrated and salty.

3. When all the water has evaporated, only solid salt crystals are left.

Salar de Uyuni is estimated to contain about **11 billion tons** (10 billion tonnes) of salt.

SUN SCREEN
SHADE BALLS

In some dry, **sunny regions**, such as in California, black plastic spheres called shade balls are floated on water reservoirs to conserve water. They prevent water from evaporating, reduce the growth of algae, and also stop sunlight from reacting with chemicals in the water and making it unfit for drinking. It is estimated that this flexible, floating layer can help reduce evaporation by 85–90 percent and last for about 25 years. But some researchers worry that the prolonged use of plastic might cause toxic reactions in the water.

In 2019, more than **780 million** people worldwide struggled to get clean drinking water.

ALGAL BLOOMS

A boat cuts through the green surface of Lake Erie in Ohio, which has become choked with algae. Under certain conditions, these aquatic organisms multiply quickly, using up oxygen in the water and producing substances harmful to fish and other life.

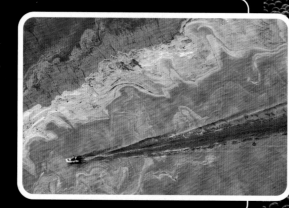

PLASTICS

Plastics have many useful properties—they are lightweight and flexible, but also strong and water resistant. Plastics are made up of molecules called polymers, long strings of smaller molecules called monomers that usually contain hydrogen and carbon. Shade balls are made of the polymer polyethylene, which is made from ethylene molecules. It is also used to make bags, bottles, and many other things.

Hydrogen atom

Carbon atom

ETHYLENE MONOMER

Hydrogen atom

Carbon atom

POLYETHYLENE (POLYTHENE) POLYMER

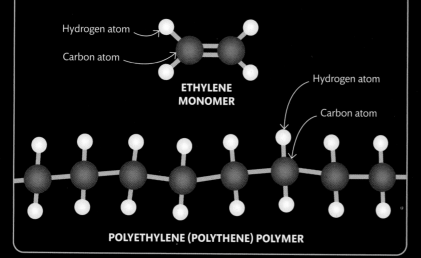

Protecting reservoirs

The state of California frequently experiences drought. Shade balls were first trialed there in 2008, when about 3 million of them were dropped into the Ivanhoe Reservoir in Los Angeles.

CLEANING DIRTY WATER

WASTE WATER TREATMENT

Billions of gallons of dirty water from industries, farms, and homes flow into drains and sewers every day. This water is a mixture of human sewage and all kinds of dangerous bacteria and chemicals, so it must be thoroughly cleaned before it can be released back into the environment. Treating waste water is essential to prevent water scarcity. The multistage process uses several physical, biological, and chemical methods to decontaminate the water and make it safe for reuse. One stage separates the solid waste from the water using a process called sedimentation.

SLUDGE CAKE

The dry solid waste left over from water treatment is called sludge cake and has its own use. Sludge cakes can be used as fertilizers to help plants grow by providing them with extra nutrients.

SEDIMENTATION

Sedimentation is a physical method of cleaning water in which heavy solid particles in a solution sink to the bottom, pulled by gravity, so they can be removed easily. When dirty water passes into a sedimentation tank (below), a sludge of solid particles, such as those from human sewage, settles at the bottom to be collected, while lighter substances such as oil and scum float to the top to be skimmed off.

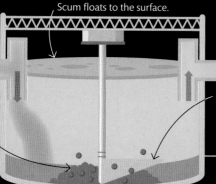

Dirty water flows into the tank.

Scum floats to the surface.

Cleaner water flows out.

Sludge settles at the bottom, so it can be collected and dried.

Turning slowly, a scraper moves solid waste to the bottom.

The waste water produced in 2020 could fill 144 million **Olympic-sized** swimming pools.

Cleaning water

This set of twelve sedimentation tanks in a wastewater treatment plant in Sha Tin, Hong Kong, works together with other treatments to clean more than 264 million gallons (1 billion liters) of sewage every day.

POWER UP!

SUPPLYING ELECTRICITY

Most electricity is generated at sites such as power stations, wind farms, or nuclear power plants before being transmitted to homes and industries through a complex network known as a power grid. These power grids are made up of interconnected cables and other infrastructure, such as transmission towers and substations, that together deliver electricity over huge distances with as little power loss as possible. Electricity travels as a current of charged particles called electrons (see page 177).

ELECTRIC CURRENT

Electric current is the movement of tiny particles called electrons. In a metal wire, electrons move about freely but in no particular direction. When this wire is connected to a source of electrical power, such as a generator or a battery, the free electrons move in a single direction.

Randomly moving electrons

Continuous flow of electrons in the same direction

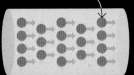

NO ELECTRIC CURRENT

ELECTRIC CURRENT

The world's **tallest** electricity pylon is in China and reaches a height of **1,214 ft** (370 m).

Powering a city

Interconnected power lines deliver electricity over large distances. Uncovered cables are suspended high above the ground on poles and towers where they do not present a hazard to people.

How current travels

The pressure that pushes electricity to travel through wires and cables is called voltage. The higher the voltage, the less energy is lost from resistance as the current travels through the power lines. At the power station, a device called a transformer increases the voltage. As it leaves the grid, another transformer decreases the voltage.

Power station

Most of the power grid is made up of aluminum cables suspended from transmission towers or pylons.

The voltage is typically boosted to 400,000 volts before it enters the power grid.

The voltage is reduced as it exits the power grid.

Home receiving electricity

A step-up transformer increases the voltage.

A step-down transformer decreases the voltage.

Cooling towers

The steam produced in a nuclear power plant must be cooled down after it passes through the turbines, so that it can enter the reactor core as cold water once again. More cold water is used to cool the steam, and in doing so becomes warm. It cools down in huge cooling towers, like these at the Novovoronezh nuclear power station in Russia.

There are currently more than **400 nuclear reactors** in operation around the globe.

ATOMIC ENERGY
NUCLEAR POWER

Nuclear power generates about 10 percent of the world's electricity. It works by harnessing the huge amount of energy stored in atoms (see page 177). This can be released by splitting apart the nucleus (center) of the atom in a reaction known as fission. Nuclear power is not a form of renewable energy, as the fuel it uses can be used up. However, its power stations do not produce harmful greenhouse gases, unlike

NUCLEAR FISSION

To release the power of the atom, a neutron is fired at the nucleus of an unstable atom, such as uranium. This splits the nucleus, releasing energy and shooting out more neutrons. They then split other nuclei, releasing even more energy and triggering a chain reaction.

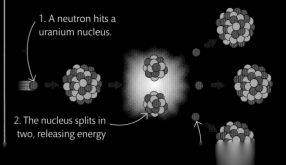

1. A neutron hits a uranium nucleus.

2. The nucleus splits in two, releasing energy

REACTOR CORE

Engineers gaze into the inactive core of a nuclear reactor where the uranium fuel rods sit surrounded by water. Uranium works well as a fuel, because it is very unstable, so its nuclei break apart easily. Some power plants use other fuels instead, such as plutonium.

From fission to electricity

Nuclear fission reactions happen in a part of a power station called the reactor core. Control rods made of graphite are lowered and raised in between rods made of uranium. The graphite absorbs neutrons and can be used to slow the chain reaction if needed. The heat of the chain reaction is used to boil water into steam, which is then sent through turbines to generate electricity.

Control rods

Uranium fuel rods

Reactor core

Steam is generated by the reaction.

Cooling water takes heat away from the steam.

The steam powers a turbine, which generates electricity.

Pylons transmit electricity to power grids.

Cooling water becomes so hot, some of it escapes as steam.

Nuclear fusion

This reactor being built in the US seeks to generate power by a nuclear reaction called fusion. In this process, the nuclei (centers) of atoms collide at such speed, they fuse together, releasing vast quantities of energy.

POWERED BY THE SUN

SOLAR ENERGY

The Sun radiates massive amounts of light and heat energy, called solar energy, which is essential for sustaining life on Earth. Solar energy can be converted into useful electrical energy with the help of technologies such as solar cells, which are arranged together to form solar panels. Solar energy is a rapidly growing source of clean, renewable energy, and it is likely to be the world's main energy source by 2050.

THE SUN

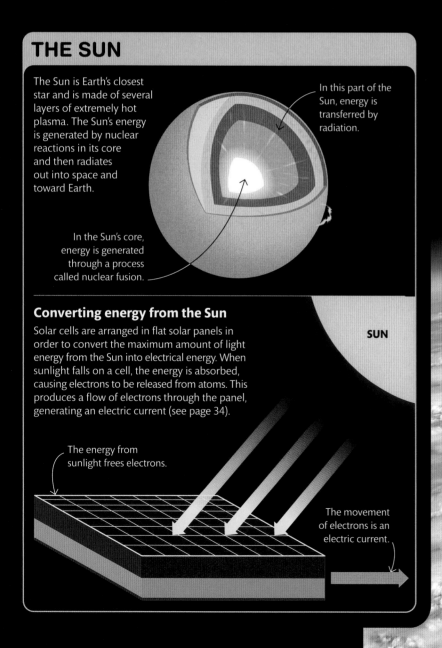

The Sun is Earth's closest star and is made of several layers of extremely hot plasma. The Sun's energy is generated by nuclear reactions in its core and then radiates out into space and toward Earth.

In this part of the Sun, energy is transferred by radiation.

In the Sun's core, energy is generated through a process called nuclear fusion.

Converting energy from the Sun

Solar cells are arranged in flat solar panels in order to convert the maximum amount of light energy from the Sun into electrical energy. When sunlight falls on a cell, the energy is absorbed, causing electrons to be released from atoms. This produces a flow of electrons through the panel, generating an electric current (see page 34).

SUN

The energy from sunlight frees electrons.

The movement of electrons is an electric current.

Each solar panel array is 112 ft (34 m) long.

Solar boat

Solar panels can be used to power transportation including the MS *Tûranor PlanetSolar*, pictured here—the world's largest solar-powered boat. It is covered with more than 5,382 sq ft (500 sq m) of solar panels.

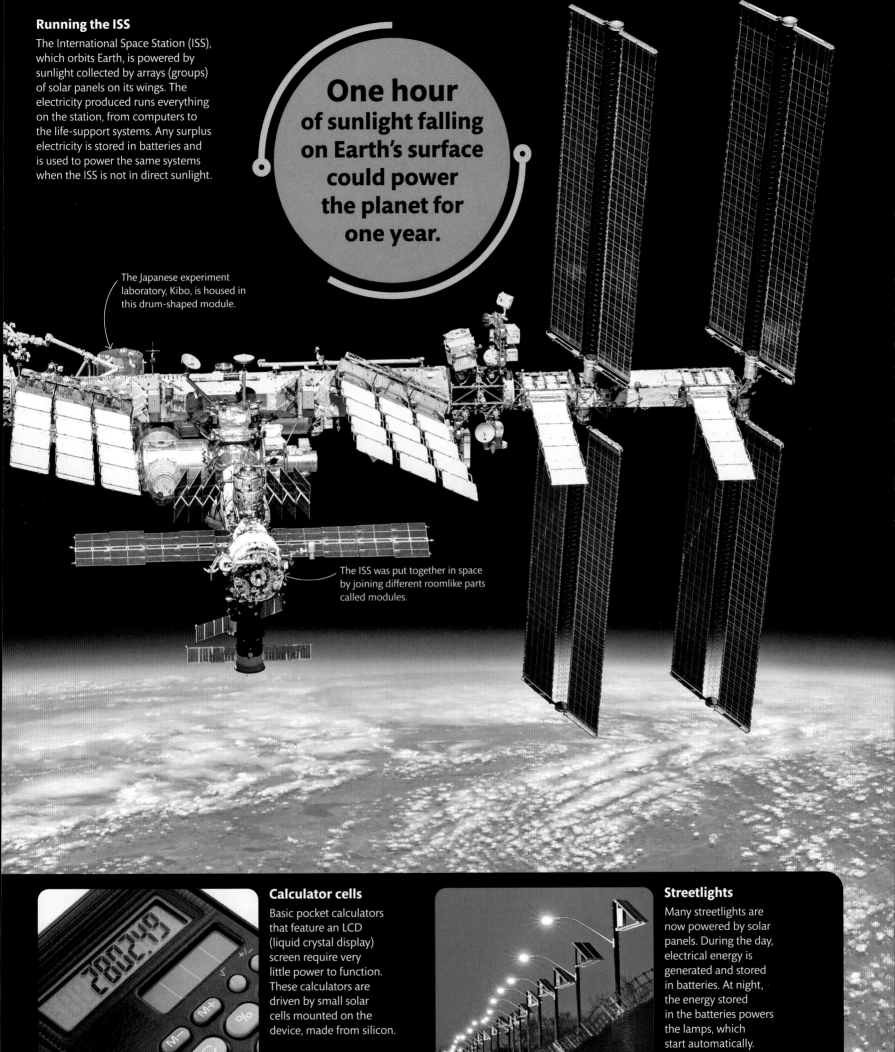

Running the ISS

The International Space Station (ISS), which orbits Earth, is powered by sunlight collected by arrays (groups) of solar panels on its wings. The electricity produced runs everything on the station, from computers to the life-support systems. Any surplus electricity is stored in batteries and is used to power the same systems when the ISS is not in direct sunlight.

One hour of sunlight falling on Earth's surface could power the planet for one year.

The Japanese experiment laboratory, Kibo, is housed in this drum-shaped module.

The ISS was put together in space by joining different roomlike parts called modules.

Calculator cells

Basic pocket calculators that feature an LCD (liquid crystal display) screen require very little power to function. These calculators are driven by small solar cells mounted on the device, made from silicon.

Streetlights

Many streetlights are now powered by solar panels. During the day, electrical energy is generated and stored in batteries. At night, the energy stored in the batteries powers the lamps, which start automatically.

ENERGY STORAGE

BIG BATTERIES

One of the biggest challenges for the renewable energy industry is producing a constant supply when wind and sunshine cannot always be guaranteed. One solution is to store energy as it is generated for later use. Gigantic rechargeable batteries, similar to those used in household electronics and electric cars (see page 89), are one way of storing this energy to ensure a continuous power supply.

PUMP POWER

Hydroelectric power stations store water's potential energy. Water stored at the top of a slope powers turbines as it flows downhill. It can be pumped back uphill when energy demands are low and stored until needed to power the turbines again.

STORING ENERGY

Energy is the ability to make things happen. It comes in many different forms, including light and heat. Energy that is stored, ready to be used, is called potential energy. Energy can be stored in many ways—for example, by lifting heavy objects, by spinning objects, or as electric charge in a battery.

A machine called a flywheel stores kinetic (movement) energy.

A suspended weight stores gravitational potential energy.

A squashed spring stores elastic potential energy.

A rechargeable battery stores electrical energy.

Super-sized storage

Long rows of large batteries at Neoen's Hornsdale Power Reserve in Australia store energy generated from wind turbines in the surrounding fields. These types of batteries are called lithium-ion batteries and can be recharged in order to be used again and again.

Neoen's Hornsdale Power Reserve can store 129 megawatt-hours of power.

AEROLEAF

Each leaflike turbine, called an Aeroleaf, is about 3 ft (1 m) tall. It rotates vertically when the wind hits its panels. As it turns, one Aeroleaf can produce up to 300 watts of electricity—enough to power about six computers.

Each mini wind turbine is made of plastic.

The trunk and branches are made of steel.

One Wind Tree produces as much electricity as the burning of **1,896 lb** (860 kg) of coal per year.

Wind Tree

Built on the outskirts of Paris, France, this unique structure is shaped like a tree, where each "leaf" acts as a mini wind turbine. One tree has about 36 turbines, which can harness gentle breezes, as well as strong gusts of wind.

HARNESSING WIND POWER

WIND TURBINES

Wind power, along with other sources such as solar power and hydropower (power from water), is a form of renewable energy—an energy source that never runs out. The Wind Tree featured here operates on a small, local level but harnesses the wind in a similar way to the giant turbines found on wind farms (see pages 46-47). Wind turbines turn the power of the wind into electrical power. The blades of a turbine rotate when the wind blows, turning a shaft and driving a machine called a generator to convert the mechanical energy of this motion into electrical energy.

MICROGENERATION

Wind turbines come in a range of sizes and designs. Mini turbines can be mounted on rooftops to generate small amounts of electricity either to meet the energy needs of a household or business or to add to the power grid.

GENERATORS

When the wind pushes on the turbines, its energy is turned into mechanical energy. This then passes to a generator, which is a machine that converts mechanical energy into electrical energy. It works using magnets. The energy from the blades spins a coil of wire around inside the magnet. This generates a flow of electrons—an electric current (see page 34). This current passes through cables to the power grid.

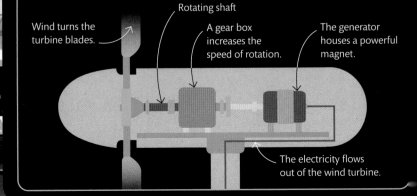

Wind turns the turbine blades.

Rotating shaft

A gear box increases the speed of rotation.

The generator houses a powerful magnet.

The electricity flows out of the wind turbine.

Wind farm on the waves

Out in the North Sea, off the coast of Denmark, sits Horns Rev—one of the world's largest offshore wind farms. Built in three phases, it has 220 turbines, which every year produce enough energy for 150,000 houses.

Growing algae

Algae are a type of organism similar to plants, shown here growing in a lab. On a large scale, they are grown in a machine called a photobioreactor, which supplies the algae with the right amount of sunlight and carbon dioxide to help them produce oil at a faster rate.

BIODIESEL BUS

DeuSEL®—the world's first biodiesel, made from the microalgae *Euglena*—powers this bus in Yokohama, Japan. The DeuSEL® project aims to develop alternative fuels that reduce carbon dioxide emissions.

GREEN ENERGY

BIOFUELS

Biofuels are fuels derived from plants, algae, or animal waste. Unlike fossil fuels, such as coal or crude oil, which formed from the remains of plants and animals that died millions of years ago, biofuels are renewable, which means they will never run out. Algae are a promising source of biofuel. When supplied with sunlight and nutrients, they produce a rich oil that can easily be turned into fuel.

FUEL FROM CORN
Corn can also be turned into biofuel. Billions of liters of corn-based fuel, called bioethanol, are produced in the US each year. Although a renewable fuel, farming biofuel crops on a large scale can have an impact on the environment and food supply.

PRODUCING BIOFUELS

Algae take in carbon dioxide from the air when they grow and produce an oil rich in carbon. The oil is extracted and then processed in a refinery to make fuel that can be used to power vehicles. When it burns, it produces the same amount of carbon dioxide it took from the air when it grew.

1. Algae use energy from sunlight and carbon dioxide from the air to grow.

2. Oil extracted from the algae is made into fuel at a refinery.

3. The fuel can be used in vehicles in the same way as gas or diesel.

4. When the fuel burns, it releases carbon dioxide into the air.

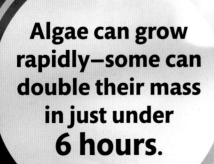

Algae can grow rapidly—some can double their mass in just under 6 hours.

BUILDING AND CREATING

Science has allowed us to build and develop many new structures and materials. From cranes that can build vast bridges and buildings, to special materials that can be used in darkness or underwater, scientists have created many things that make our lives easier. Science also helps us recycle materials such as glass and aluminum, reducing pollution and conserving precious resources.

VERTICAL FORESTS
ECO BUILDINGS

In many places around the world, vehicles and industry emit harmful gases and particles of pollution in the air that can lead to health risks when inhaled. Some eco-friendly buildings in cities are designed to act as urban air purifiers. The towers of Bosco Verticale (meaning "vertical forest") in Milan, Italy, have many plants on their outsides. These catch polluting particles and absorb carbon dioxide gas to use in a process called photosynthesis. This gas contributes to climate change (see page 156).

SMOG-FREE TOWER
This aluminum tower in Rotterdam, the Netherlands, acts like a vacuum cleaner for smog. Designed to work in parks, it sucks up air, removes tiny polluting particles, and releases clean air. Highly energy-efficient, it uses almost the same amount of power as a coffee maker.

PHOTOSYNTHESIS

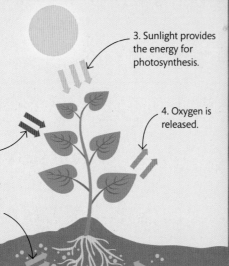

Plants need carbon dioxide to grow. Their leaves convert it into energy and oxygen using water and sunlight in a reaction called photosynthesis. A plant's waxy leaves also have a big and sticky surface area for trapping very small polluting particles.

3. Sunlight provides the energy for photosynthesis.

4. Oxygen is released.

2. Carbon dioxide enters the leaf.

1. Water and minerals are absorbed through the roots and transported up the stem.

Living buildings
These solar-powered residential towers are "living buildings"—the vegetation growing on them reduces humidity and helps keep the buildings cool in summer. They also attract many birds and butterflies.

About **800** trees; **5,000** shrubs; and **15,000** other plants cover the buildings.

Seeing heat

This image of a house was taken with a special infrared camera (see pages 184–185) that shows different temperatures as different colors. It shows that the house is losing heat through the walls to its colder surroundings. Knowing where to insulate helps save heating and cooling costs.

Blue shows that the roof is cool, possibly because it has insulation.

Red indicates warmth and that heat from inside the house is escaping.

Without insulation, a house may lose up to 60 percent of the heat inside it.

COLD   HOT

TRAPPING HEAT

HOUSE INSULATION

Heat always moves from warmer to cooler places.
It is easily lost from our homes to the outside air through
roofs, walls, doors, and windows. Insulation is a way of
reducing the rate of heat lost from the warmer insides
of a house to its cooler surroundings during cold
winters. In the same way, insulation keeps the house
cool in the summer. The roof and walls of modern
homes often include a layer of materials through
which heat passes slowly, such as foam, fiberglass
and plastic, making them more energy-efficient

KEEPING COOL
In the hot climate of
New Mexico, these
homes were designed to
stay cool on the inside
by using adobe bricks—
one of the oldest building
materials in the world. They
are made of clay mixed
with straw or dung.

HEAT TRANSFER

Heat naturally flows from a hot object or area to cooler objects or surroundings. It is
transferred in three different ways. Some objects give off heat as waves directly into the
air, which is called radiation. Heat can also travel through solids by conduction and
through liquids and gases through a process called convection. When water is
heated in a saucepan, the heat travels through it in convection currents.

The cooler
water sinks to
be heated up
by convection.

The warm water
becomes less
dense and rises.

The stove's
flame radiates
heat in the air.

Heat passes
through the pan
to the handle
by conduction.

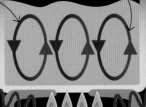

Icy base

The Halley VI Antarctic Research Station monitors the atmosphere in one of the harshest environments on Earth. The base can withstand temperatures as low as −67°F (−55°C) and has long legs to keep its modules above any snow.

Each suspender rope can bear as much weight as 500,000 lb (225,000 kg).

Thick steel cables support the long suspenders.

The Golden Gate Bridge has 500 suspenders, and the wires in its cables could circle Earth three times.

CREATING CROSSINGS
SUSPENSION BRIDGES

High and mighty

The world-famous Golden Gate Bridge spans a 1-mile (1.6-km) stretch of seawater, connecting the city of San Francisco with Marin County. When it opened in 1937, the bridge was the tallest and the longest suspension bridge in the world.

The vertical pillars stand 746 ft (227 m) tall and are anchored deep in the seabed.

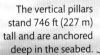

A bridge is a structure that supports a road, allowing people and vehicles to cross over rivers, seas, valleys, and other obstacles. There are many different types of bridges but the design with the largest span is the suspension bridge. This is held up by long chains called suspenders which are supported by thick cables and tall pillars. Suspension bridges are not as rigid as other types, which means they can withstand forces such as earthquakes.

CABLE-STAYED BRIDGE

Another type of bridge that uses cables to support a road is the cable-stayed bridge. Here, the cables are attached directly to the road. This picture shows the world's highest cable-stayed bridge in Ghuizhou, China.

TENSION AND COMPRESSION

The weight of the road and the traffic stretches the suspenders and cables—they are in tension, and they pull back, like a rubber band does, supporting the road. Where they are attached to the pillars, the cables pull downward, and the pillars are in compression. Like any object under compression, the pillars push back, supporting the whole bridge.

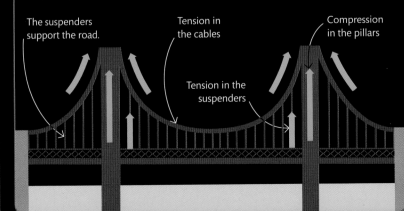

The suspenders support the road.

Tension in the cables

Compression in the pillars

Tension in the suspenders

LOAD LIFTERS
CRANES

Building bridges and skyscrapers means heavy loads need to be lifted. This can be done by large machines called cranes, which make use of levers and pulleys. Along with screws and wheels-and-axles, pulleys and levers are all examples of simple machines—devices that can change the direction of forces and convert large forces into small ones or small forces into large ones. In nearly all cranes, a system of pulleys—wheels with rope passing over them—is mainly responsible for lifting the load.

WRENCHES

A wrench, which is used to turn nuts and bolts, is a type of simple machine called a lever. Levers turn about a fixed point called a fulcrum (here at the head of the wrench). Pushing on the wrench away from the fulcrum and farther down the wrench's long handle increases the force at the fulcrum.

PULLEYS

A pulley makes it easier to lift a load. With a single pulley, you can lift a load upward by pulling downward on a rope instead—an easier action. When two or more pulleys are combined by connecting them with a single rope—also called a block and tackle—a much greater load can be lifted than the force with which the rope is pulled.

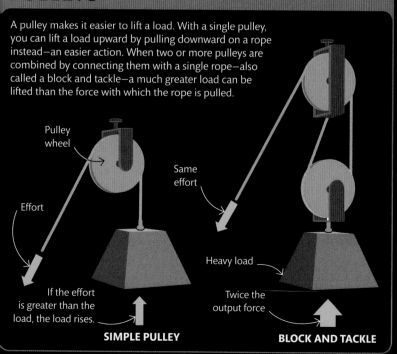

Pulley wheel

Effort

Same effort

If the effort is greater than the load, the load rises.

Heavy load

Twice the output force

SIMPLE PULLEY

BLOCK AND TACKLE

Cables help lift the arms of the crane.

The huge metal arms act as levers, helping raise and lower the loads.

These tower cranes are attached to the bridge and help move objects around the site.

Lifting high

An enormous floating crane lifts a large section of the Zhoushan-Daishan bridge in China, which was under construction in 2021. These cranes require two separate systems of pulleys to handle their loads. While one system lifts the load, the other lifts the arms that are carrying the load.

The long, thick metal ropes pass over many pulley wheels inside the block and tackle.

This concrete girder will form part of the bridge.

FLOATING PLATFORM

Cranes with huge metal arms that are mounted on boats and used to perform tasks in water are called floating sheerlegs. They are often used in construction, for loading and unloading cargo from ships, and to fish out sunken wrecks from the bottom of the sea.

This crane can lift girders each weighing **2,000 tons** (1,800 tonnes)—the same weight as 400 adult elephants.

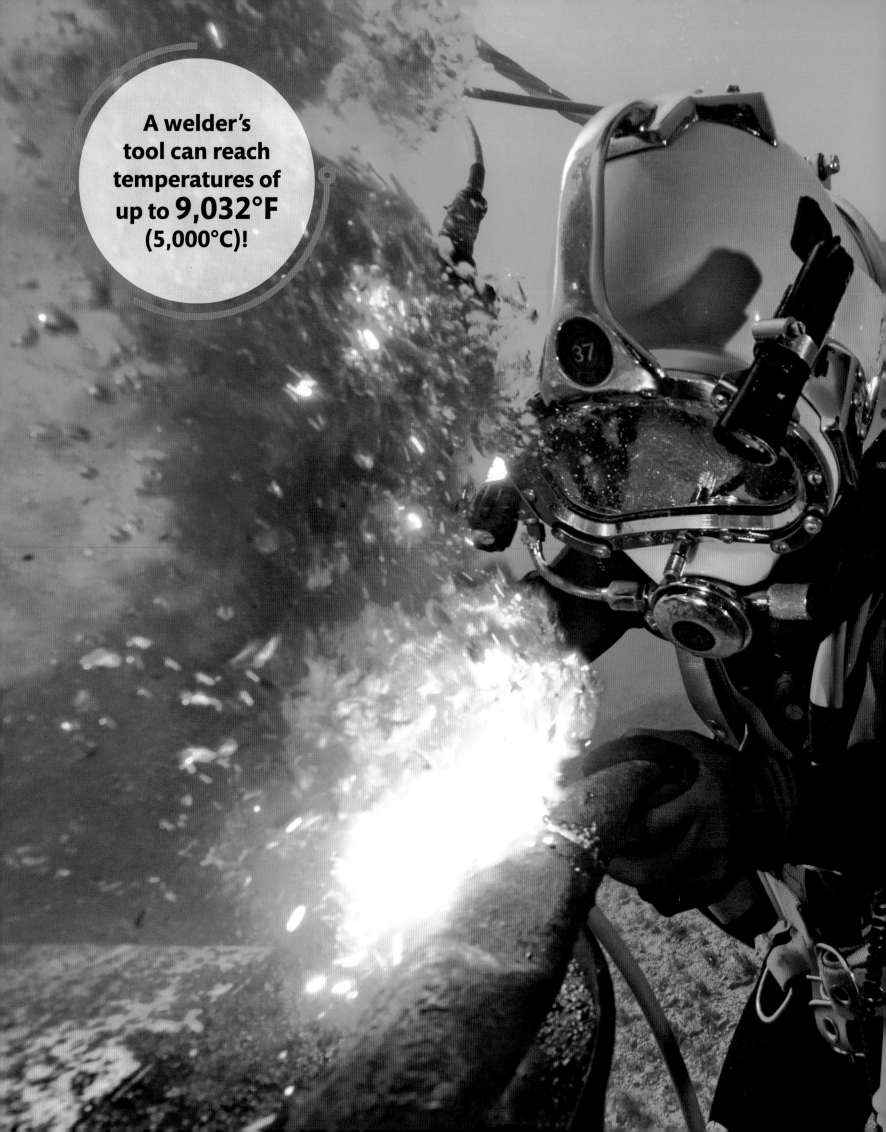

A welder's tool can reach temperatures of up to **9,032°F** (5,000°C)!

Welding under pressure

At a training school in the South of France, bubbles form in the water as a student diver begins cutting through metal. The welding process actually takes place within a waterproof, gaseous bubble, which naturally forms around the welder's tool.

MARINE REPAIRS

UNDERWATER WELDING

Welding is the process of joining metals by melting the two separate parts and allowing them to fuse as they cool. It has an important role in construction and sometimes needs to be done underwater—for instance, to make repairs to offshore oil rigs or to fix broken parts of a ship. Underwater welding takes in energy from its surroundings as it happens in what is known as an endothermic process. Safety is crucial, as the metals are melted using electricity.

CONDUCTORS

Water is a conductor of electricity, meaning it allows electricity to pass through it easily. Saltwater is an even better conductor. A saltwater solution can be used to complete a circuit. As underwater welding is often done in saltwater, electric shock is a big risk.

ENDOTHERMIC VS. EXOTHERMIC

Chemical reactions and some processes can be endothermic or exothermic. Oxy-fuel welding (shown here) is different to underwater welding and uses a hot flame to melt metals. This is an example of an endothermic process—one that takes in heat. When the metals solidify, they give out heat to their surroundings. This is an exothermic process.

Welding torch tip

Joint forming between two welded sections.

As the metal melts, it takes in energy.

ENDOTHERMIC

As the metal sets, it gives off energy.

EXOTHERMIC

CUTTING TOOLS

DIAMOND DRILLS

Diamond is a solid form of carbon (an element). An element is a substance made up of only one type of atom. Natural diamonds formed billions of years ago, under high pressures and temperatures deep within Earth, but nowadays they can also be made synthetically. Although it is best known as a shiny gemstone, diamond is the hardest naturally occurring material, a property which gives it a range of uses in industry and manufacturing.

CUT DIAMONDS

Diamonds have always been valued as gemstones. Rough stones are shaped and carefully cut to create many tiny surfaces called facets. When light enters the stone, these facets cause it to bounce around and split into different colors, creating a sparkly effect.

FORMS OF CARBON

Pure carbon atoms can join together in different ways. The two best-known forms are diamond and graphite, but in 1985, a third type was discovered, called buckminsterfullerene. Their different structures give these substances unique properties. Graphite is soft and often used in pencils, while diamond is so hard it can cut through concrete.

DIAMOND	GRAPHITE	BUCKMINSTERFULLERENE
	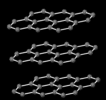	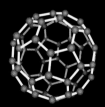
Atoms in diamond form a strong pyramid shape.	In graphite, atoms are arranged in layers that slide over each other.	Sixty carbon atoms are arranged in a ball in this form of carbon.

Diamond drill
Because of its hardness, diamond is used in many tools. In this image, a drill tipped with diamond polishes blocks of metal. Diamond is also added to the blades of saws in order to cut through tough materials such as steel.

Diamonds may have been used **6,000 years ago** to polish prehistoric axes.

Lidar

Lidar technology (light detection and ranging) works by reflecting laser beams off a target object. This provides data so a computer can build a 3D model of the target. Self-driving cars use lidar, among other tools, to navigate through their surroundings.

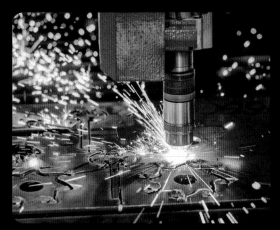

Laser cutting

Laser beams can be used to cut materials. The narrow, powerful beam is pointed at the material, causing it to heat up. The material in the beam's path melts, burns, or vaporizes, leaving a clean edge.

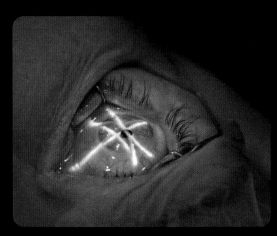

Delicate surgery

Lasers have many surgical applications. In laser eye surgery, an ultraviolet laser is used to remove a thin layer of the eye, reshaping it so that the eye can focus light better.

Laser-guided telescopes

The power and precision of laser beams means they don't spread out very much. At the Very Large Telescope in Chile, astronomers use lasers that help guide computers mapping the movement of stars.

Laser beams from Earth have been **reflected** back from a panel left on the **Moon** by astronauts.

LIGHT POWER
LASERS

In 1960, American scientist Theodore Maiman built a device that could emit a narrow, powerful beam of single-color light—the world's first laser. The name stands for "light amplification by stimulated emission of radiation." In a laser device, a material is supplied with energy. This makes the atoms of the material release energy in the form of light waves that travel as a straight beam of light. The properties of laser light give it many applications, such as in surgery, telescopes, and communications.

LASER LIGHT

Light is a form of energy that travels as waves (see page 184). Light waves from most sources have a mix of different wavelengths and colors that move out of step. However, waves of laser light have identical wavelengths and travel perfectly in step with each other. These properties mean laser light is very intense and its energy can be easily concentrated onto specific objects.

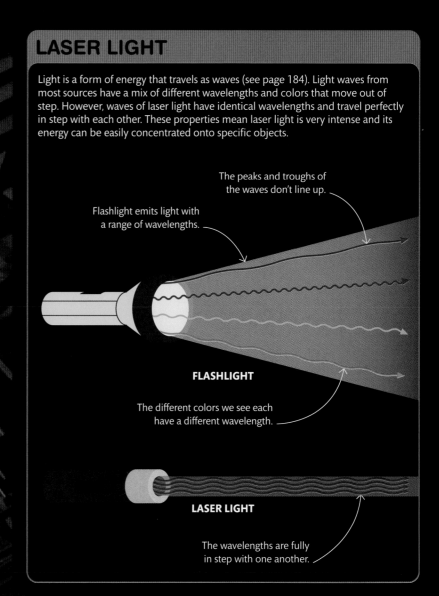

The peaks and troughs of the waves don't line up.

Flashlight emits light with a range of wavelengths.

FLASHLIGHT

The different colors we see each have a different wavelength.

LASER LIGHT

The wavelengths are fully in step with one another.

Natural vs synthetic

A frog sits inside a water droplet on a lotus leaf in a pond in Nepal. Lotus leaves are known for their hydrophobic (water-repellent) properties, which stop water from sinking into the leaves. Instead, it forms spherical droplets on the surface. The attractions between the water molecules in these droplets are so strong, they can trap tiny creatures like this frog. The bumpy surface of the human-made material on the right has been designed to mimic that of the lotus leaf to make it waterproof.

The lotus leaf has also **inspired** the design of **self-cleaning paint!**

BUMPY SURFACE

Water does not wet a lotus leaf because the leaf surface is covered in tiny, pointy structures and coated in natural waxes. The ridged surface reduces how much of the leaf is in contact with the water.

STAYING DRY

WATER-REPELLENT MATERIALS

Scientists are often inspired by nature when creating new materials, and many plants and animals have natural waterproof features that they have sought to copy. Sheep secrete an oily substance called lanolin that keeps rain off their wool, while lotus leaves have a waxy coating and a special structure that makes them especially water-resistant. By mimicking these features, scientists have created water-repellent materials that act as a barrier, so that water sits on top of them due to its natural surface tension.

HIGH AND DRY

Waterproof materials are used to make clothing worn by walkers and mountaineers. One type of material, called Gore-Tex®, is breathable, as well as waterproof. It is made of many layers and has tiny holes to let out water vapor without letting in droplets of liquid water.

SURFACE TENSION

Water sits in droplets on waterproof materials, because water particles have a greater attraction to each other than they do to the air or the material's surface. As a result, water droplets shrink to form a ball, or a sphere—a shape with the smallest possible surface area. This property of water is called surface tension and can be seen in dewdrops on leaves and raindrops on windowpanes.

The forces attracting the molecules cause the water droplet to take on a spherical shape.

Water molecules are strongly attracted to each other.

The droplet sits on a waterproof surface without sinking into it.

HIGH VISIBILITY

REFLECTIVE MATERIALS

High-viz, or high-visibility, clothing is essential for cyclists and people who work in safety-critical jobs such as construction. It allows them to be easily seen when it is dark or if there is a lot of activity going on around them. High-viz clothing is made using materials that are retroflective (reflect light directly back to its source), making the object much easier to see. These materials are also used to make road signs easy to see even in the dark.

Easy to spot
The retroreflective strips on this child's bicycle and clothing shine brightly in an oncoming car's headlights, making them easy to spot on a dark winter evening.

REFLECTION

Most objects scatter light in all directions when it hits them, but when light bounces off shiny or reflective surfaces, it bounces back in a predictable way. The reflected light makes the same angle as the incoming, or incident, light.

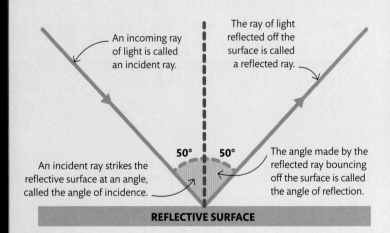

An incoming ray of light is called an incident ray.

The ray of light reflected off the surface is called a reflected ray.

An incident ray strikes the reflective surface at an angle, called the angle of incidence.

50° 50°

The angle made by the reflected ray bouncing off the surface is called the angle of reflection.

REFLECTIVE SURFACE

Retroreflection

Retroreflective surfaces are covered with tiny glass beads or prisms, which reflect light back in the same direction it comes from. Retroreflective materials cause light to be precisely directed back to its source so the object appears to shine brightly.

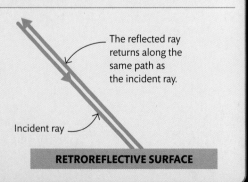

The reflected ray returns along the same path as the incident ray.

Incident ray

RETROREFLECTIVE SURFACE

The eyes of a cat appear to shine in the dark because of a retroreflective layer in its eyes.

PRISMATIC TAPE

An optical prism refracts, or bends, light, and prismatic tape uses this property. It contains a layer of small prisms called "cube-corners," which direct light back to its source. This type of tape is used on vehicles and equipment, and when a light falls on it, it shines brightly.

Turkish freediver Şahika Ercümen suits up and prepares to dive between two icebergs near Galindez Island, Antarctica. Wetsuits can have varying thicknesses of neoprene for diving in waters of different temperatures.

STAYING WARM IN THE WATER

WETSUITS

Even on a hot day, water can steal enough heat from the human body to give a person hypothermia (a dangerous drop in body temperature). Unlike marine animals such as whales, which have a layer of fat to stay warm, humans need artificial coverings such as wetsuits to stay warm in cold water. Wetsuits let water in through the neck, sleeves, and legs, but very little heat can escape through the material, so the thin layer of water and the body keep warmer for longer.

A 0.28-in (7-mm) thick wetsuit can keep a diver alive in **water as cold as 50°F (10°C).**

FLUFFY COAT
Animals from cold, harsh environments are equipped with their own insulation. Polar bears rely on their thick fur and fat to survive in the freezing cold of the Arctic, with the thick layers providing an insulating effect similar to that of a wetsuit.

INSULATING MATERIALS

The secret to a wetsuit's insulating properties is a layer of material called neoprene. Neoprene is a synthetic (human-made) form of rubber made into a foam with many bubbles of air inside, which slow the loss of heat. A thin layer of water also gets trapped between the suit and body and is warmed up by a diver's body heat. Together, the layer of warm water and the neoprene layer help keep the diver warm in the cold water.

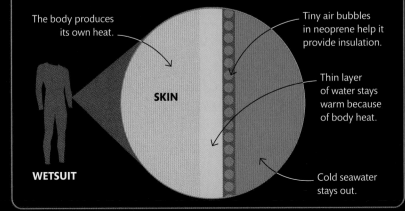

The body produces its own heat.

Tiny air bubbles in neoprene help it provide insulation.

SKIN

Thin layer of water stays warm because of body heat.

WETSUIT

Cold seawater stays out.

GLASSBLOWING

In glassblowing, a long tube is used to blow air into hot, softened glass to form a bubble, which can then be shaped, as seen here. Specialized pieces of laboratory glassware and expensive decorative items such as vases are still made today using this technique.

Gold salts can be added to molten glass to give it a rich ruby-red color.

New from old

At this factory in Italy, extremely hot blobs of used glass are shaped into new bottles. Machines mix small pieces of crushed glass with other raw materials before heating it to more than 2,732°F (1,500°C), producing a new bottle. Glass is infinitely recyclable, so this process can happen many times.

SEE-THROUGH SOLID

MAKING GLASS

People have been making glass objects for at least 6,000 years. Sand is one of the main substances used to make glass. When melted and formed into a solid, glass has many useful properties—it is hard when cool but is easily shaped when heated, it doesn't react with many chemicals, and it is transparent. As a result, glass can be used to make a variety of objects, such as bottles and jars, laboratory equipment, car windshields, and even computer screens.

TRANSPARENCY

We see objects when light bounces or reflects off them into our eyes. Most glass is transparent, meaning visible light passes through and we can see things on the other side. Frosted glass is translucent, only allowing some light through. Opaque materials don't allow any light through.

TRANSPARENT

Transparent materials, such as glass, allow almost all light to pass through. Only a little is reflected back, which allows us to see the surface of the glass.

TRANSLUCENT

Translucent materials, such as frosted glass, block some light. The light that passes through is scattered by tiny indentations on the surface of the glass.

OPAQUE

Opaque objects, such as wood or metal, reflect or absorb all the light that falls on them.

REDUCING PLASTIC WASTE

BIODEGRADABLE MATERIALS

It is estimated that in 2017, a **million** plastic bottles were bought **every** minute.

Plastics have many useful properties—they are cheap to produce, lightweight, and hard-wearing. But the durability of plastic is a problem when you want to dispose of it. Plastics are human-made and tend to break down into smaller pieces, polluting the environment for decades, if not longer. Scientists are developing biodegradable plastics, to be easily broken down by microbes such as fungi and bacteria, as well as new alternative materials.

PROBLEM PLASTIC

Although plastic can be recycled, it is estimated that only 9 percent is. About 12 percent is incinerated and 79 percent is dumped in landfill sites or the ocean. More than 7.9 million tons (7.2 million tonnes) of plastic end up in the ocean each year, polluting the marine environment.

RECYCLING PLASTICS

There are many different types of plastic. Some are more easy to recycle than others, so it is important to know the difference to help you dispose of them correctly. Best of all, avoid using plastics whenever you can—for example, drinking from a reusable water bottle and using paper straws and cups.

EASILY RECYCLED

Polyethylene terephthalate (PET) is a common type of plastic used to make most plastic bottles.

High-density polyethylene (HDPE) is a strong plastic found in jars and shampoo bottles.

LESS EASILY RECYCLED

Polystyrene is lightweight and can be used to make cups and packing materials.

Low-density polyethylene (LDPE) is very soft and flexible and is often used in plastic bags.

Plants under plastic

These corn plants are keeping warm and moist as they grow under biodegradable plastic at a farm in Wales, UK. Over time, the plastic breaks down naturally and its harmless remains are consumed by microbes in the soil.

Compostable bottles

A compostable plastic made from sugarcane has been used to create these plastic bottles in a factory in France. They will decompose into water, carbon dioxide, and humus, an ingredient of soil.

Edible cups

Single-use plastic cups are a big source of plastic waste. One solution is to produce them from materials that can be eaten. In 2016, the Indonesian brand Evoware used seaweed to produce colorful edible cups, called Ello Jello.

Jute bags

Jute is a plant-based fiber that can be woven into materials such as burlap and hessian. Unlike cotton, jute can be grown with little more than rainwater, requiring almost no fertilizer or pesticides, making it a more environmentally friendly option.

TRANSFORMING WASTE

ALUMINUM RECYCLING

Aluminum is one of the most recycled and valuable materials in our recycling bins. What makes the metal so useful are its physical properties, which allow it to be molded into new shapes easily. Products made of aluminum can be collected, melted, and easily made into new ones. Recycling aluminum from products, such as old cans, foil, and even old car parts, uses nearly 95 percent less energy than making aluminum from its raw ore.

RECYCLED PRODUCTS

Over two-thirds of drink cans in the US and Europe are made of recycled aluminum. Every year, more than 40 billion cans are recycled in the US and about 31 billion cans are recycled in Europe.

PROPERTIES OF ALUMINUM

Aluminum belongs to a group of materials called metals, which all have similar properties. Like all other metals, aluminum allows heat and electricity to pass through it easily. Like most other metals, aluminum is strong and has a shiny silver surface. But unlike many metals, aluminum does not easily corrode.

Ductility

Aluminum can be stretched into wires without breaking or losing its strength.

Malleability

Its malleability allows aluminum to be hammered into new shapes such as sheets.

Strength

Strong and long-lasting, aluminum can resist a force without breaking.

1 Sorting
Aluminum cans are collected and taken to the recycling plant, where they are checked to make sure they don't contain anything else, such as steel, plastic, or paper containers.

2 Crushing and baling
Cans take up a lot of space, so once sorted, they are crushed flat and then pressed into bales. This process compacts the cans down to a fraction of their original volume and makes them easier to move and store.

3 Melting
The bales are then shredded, and any inks on them are removed by blasting them with hot air at a searing 930°F (500°C). The shreds are melted in a furnace at 1,380°F (750°C), poured into molds, and cooled with water.

A single ingot can be 50 ft (15 m) long and contain enough metal to make **1.5 million** cans.

4 Preparing ingots
The cooled aluminum is molded into blocks called ingots, stored here in large piles. Ingots can be heated and rolled into thin sheets, which are used to make new cans or other products.

Temple of a million bottles
Thailand's eco-friendly temple Wat Pa Maha Chedi Kaew was built using 1.5 million reused glass bottles. The bottles were collected from locals who were encouraged by the temple's monks to reuse them.

Preserving food and medicine

Dry ice is often used to keep food frozen while it is being transported long distances and can also keep medicine at the right temperature. It turns to gaseous carbon dioxide as it defrosts, which keeps away mold, insects, or other pests.

Creating fog

The clouds of smoke used to create effects at concerts and in theaters are produced using fog machines. In these machines, pieces of dry ice are dropped into hot or boiling water. The dry ice turns the evaporating water into fog, which is then blown out using fans.

Dry ice blasting

Dry ice pellets can be blasted at surfaces to clean them. As they hit, they scrub the surface of dirt and impurities before turning into gas and leaving no residue behind.

SUPERCOOLANT

DRY ICE

Frozen carbon dioxide gas is called dry ice, because it does not melt into a liquid when heated, but changes directly into a gas in a process known as sublimation. Dry ice is very cold, with a temperature as low as −109.3°F (−78.5°C). This property makes it very useful for keeping things cool, especially in the storage and shipping of food, medicine, and other supplies that spoil easily. When it becomes a gas, dry ice can be used to cool objects without wetting them and is also used to create fun special effects.

Dry ice pellets must be handled with insulated gloves to avoid **frostbite** or **cold burns.**

Cooling car cockpits

Formula 1 cars have powerful engines that produce a lot of heat. During a race, air cools the moving car, but if the engine is running while the car is not moving, the cockpit becomes very hot for the driver. Dry ice is sometimes used to cool the cockpit. Here, cold carbon dioxide that has sublimed from dry ice is being pumped into the cockpit of British driver Jenson Button's car at the 2011 Singapore Grand Prix.

PROPERTIES OF GASES

Gases, liquids, and solids are the three different states of matter (see page 25). Each state has different properties. In gases, the molecules are far apart and free to move around. Gases are also very sensitive to pressure and temperature. A gas such as carbon dioxide can be made into solid dry ice when high pressure is applied to it, squeezing the space between the gas molecules and tightly packing them together.

Easy to compress

The molecules in a gas move quickly in all directions. They can be forced into a smaller space.

Expand to fill up space

The molecules are randomly arranged and will expand to fill any space they are in.

Free-moving particles

The molecules in a gas have higher energy than those in a liquid or solid and move freely.

Black
ink layer

The spacing and size
of the yellow dots is
varied to produce a
bolder or paler color.

CREATING COLOR

PRINTING

Pure magenta
is purplish red.
Magenta mixed with
yellow makes red.

Cyan mixed
with magenta
makes blue.
Cyan is actually
a greenish-
blue color.

By using different
amounts of cyan,
magenta, yellow, and
black, any color
can be created.

Our eyes see colors when light of different wavelengths enters them. When printing in color, printers use four inks—cyan, magenta, yellow, and key (black). Any color can be reproduced by mixing these CMYK colors together. Each colored image in this book is built up using tiny printed dots of each of these colors. On a computer or television screen, colored images are produced by mixing different colors—red, green, and blue.

Four-color process

When printing, computers produce four layers of the same image—one for each of the four CMYK colors. Putting the four layers together, a beautiful, vivid image is created, such as this photograph of coral and fish in the Red Sea.

This image is made of tiny dots of each CMYK color.

COLOR MIXING

Color pictures on paper are made by mixing paints or printing inks. This is called subtractive mixing. When light lands on images of a certain color, they absorb (or subtract) a specific color of that light and the other colors left are reflected back to us. The mixture of them results in the final color we see. Electronic devices, however, make color by mixing light and instead use additive mixing, where red, blue, and green light are added together to produce different colors.

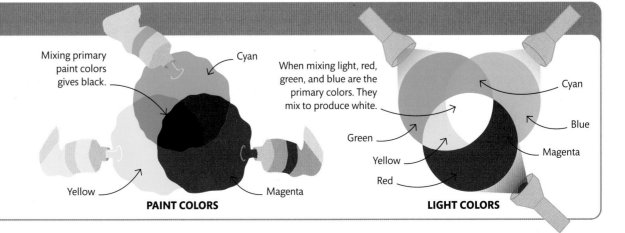

Mixing primary paint colors gives black.

Cyan

Yellow

Magenta

PAINT COLORS

When mixing light, red, green, and blue are the primary colors. They mix to produce white.

Green

Yellow

Red

Cyan

Blue

Magenta

LIGHT COLORS

TRAVELING AND CONNECTING

The world has become smaller as we are able to travel farther and faster with the help of science. We explore the digital world through the internet and travel across the real world in silent electric cars, super-fast maglev trains, and even colorful hot air balloons. Rockets and rovers take us even further, bringing us information from other planets.

Extreme E racing
The electric SUV ODYSSEY 21 is designed to compete in Extreme E races. Started in 2021, this new motorsport involves racing electric off-road vehicles in remote locations to raise awareness of climate change.

CLEAN AND FAST
ELECTRIC CARS

Rather than running on a tank filled with gas or diesel, electric cars get their power by plugging into a socket and taking electricity from the grid (see pages 34–35). They store the electricity in big rechargeable batteries that power an electric motor. Electric cars emit no exhaust fumes or harmful greenhouse gases (see page 156)

MOON BUGGY
American Astronaut Eugene A. Cernan drove a Lunar Roving Vehicle or "moon buggy" on the Moon in 1972. This electric vehicle ran on two nonrechargeable batteries and could travel 22.3 miles

BATTERIES

Batteries have positive (+) and negative (-) ends (terminals). When the two terminals are joined in a circuit, a chemical reaction inside the battery sends an electric current (see page 177) around the circuit, powering the devices connected in the circuit.

A circuit is a loop of wire through which electricity flows.

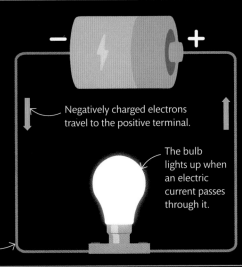

Negatively charged electrons travel to the positive terminal.

The bulb lights up when an electric current passes through it.

How electric cars work

Electric cars don't have many of the parts found in traditional vehicles, such as fuel tanks or engines. Instead, an electric car has an electric motor powered by large battery packs. The motor turns electrical energy into mechanical energy, which turns the wheels.

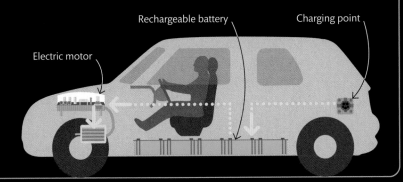

Rechargeable battery

Charging point

Electric motor

Driverless racing

The electric Robocar competes in Roborace, a competition for self-driving cars. Each team has the same vehicle but writes their own software. In 2019, Robocar broke the world record for fastest autonomous car, with a speed of 175 mph (282 km/h).

SPEEDY TRAVEL
MAGLEV TRAINS

Maglev (magnetic levitation) trains have no engine or wheels. Instead, they use powerful magnets to float in the air above the track, while more magnets on the track pull them forwards. The lack of friction between the train and the track allows the train to speed up quickly. The train and tracks also undergo less wear and tear, so they need little maintenance compared to conventional trains.

Floating in air

Most maglev trains use special types of magnets called electromagnets to levitate themselves. These are located at the side of and underneath the train and repel other electromagnets on the guiding rail. To propel the train, an electric current is passed through coils into the guiding rail. This creates a changing magnetic field so that the magnets on the train are constantly being repelled and attracted, moving it forward.

The Shanghai Maglev train is **the fastest train** in the world, with **a top speed of 267 mph (430 km/h).**

The nose of the train is curved to produce an aerodynamic shape.

The guiding rail is what the train travels over. The train body wraps around it.

MAGNETS

Magnets are objects that attract other magnets or things containing iron or other magnetic metals, such as nickel and cobalt. A magnet has two ends called a north and south pole. When opposite poles of a magnet are held near each other, they attract. When the same poles are held close to each other, they repel. The area around a magnet, in which magnetic forces are exerted, is called a magnetic field.

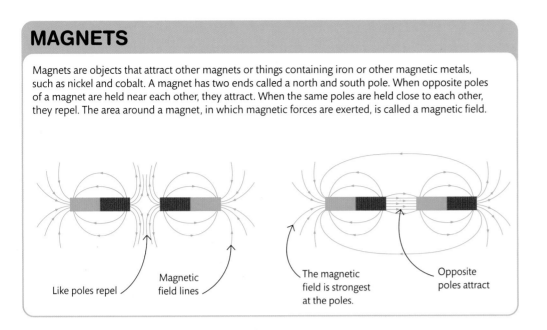

Like poles repel

Magnetic field lines

The magnetic field is strongest at the poles.

Opposite poles attract

ELECTROMAGNETS

An electromagnet is made when electricity is passed through a wire, often coiled around an iron core, causing it to produce a magnetic field. Huge electromagnets are used to lift heavy objects, such as scrap metal.

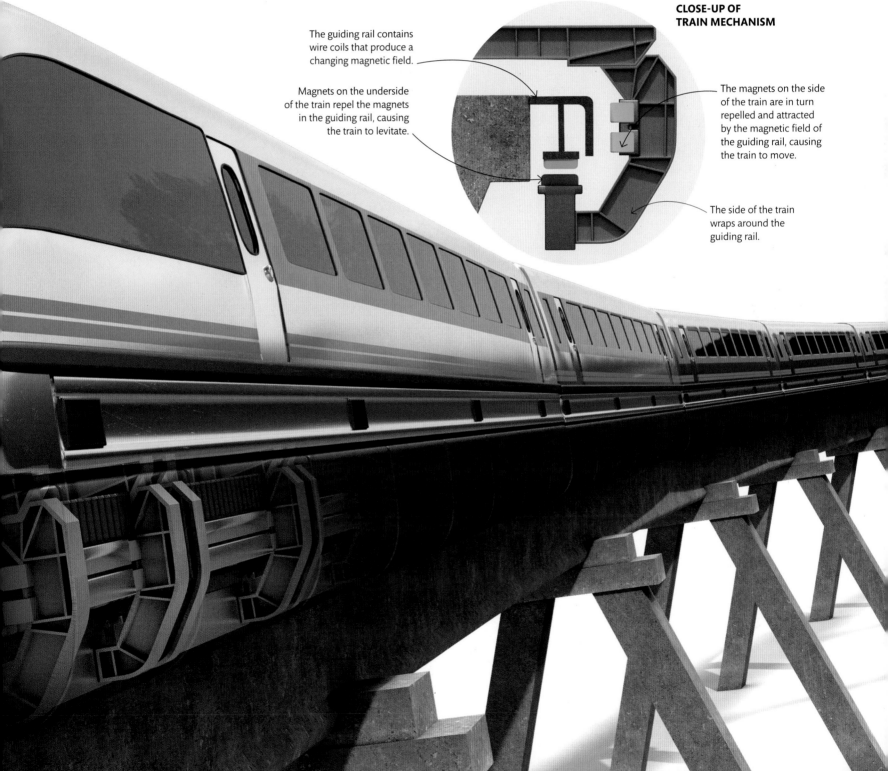

CLOSE-UP OF TRAIN MECHANISM

The guiding rail contains wire coils that produce a changing magnetic field.

Magnets on the underside of the train repel the magnets in the guiding rail, causing the train to levitate.

The magnets on the side of the train are in turn repelled and attracted by the magnetic field of the guiding rail, causing the train to move.

The side of the train wraps around the guiding rail.

FLOATING HIGH

HOT AIR BALLOONS

Unlike speedy planes, hot air balloons float across the sky slowly. French brothers Joseph-Michel and Jacques-Étienne Montgolfier carried out the first balloon flight in 1793 with a balloon made of silk and paper. Hot air balloons today are made of materials such as nylon or polyester, with a flameproof skirt at the bottom for safety. They are filled with hot air using a burner. As the air warms up, the particles move faster, spread out, and take up more space, making the air less dense than the cooler air outside the balloon. This generates a force called upthrust, which causes the balloon to rise up in the sky.

FLYING AIRSHIPS

Airships, like this one in Germany, are filled with helium gas. Just like hot air, helium is less dense than the air in which it floats. Airships have propellers and rudders, which direct them through the air, while a hot air balloon flies in whichever direction the wind blows.

UPTHRUST

An upward force, called upthrust, pushes a hot air balloon upward. Upthrust is produced by air pressure, which pushes in all directions but is stronger below the balloon than above it.

2. Air inside the balloon heats up and becomes less dense than the air outside.

3. Air pressure pushing from the bottom of the balloon produces the force called upthrust.

1. The burners produce a flame, which heats the air inside the balloon.

4. The balloon floats when the weight of the balloon is less than or equal to the upthrust on the balloon.

UPTHRUST

WEIGHT

The world's largest passenger hot air balloon is **131 ft** (40 m) tall and can carry **32 people** at a time.

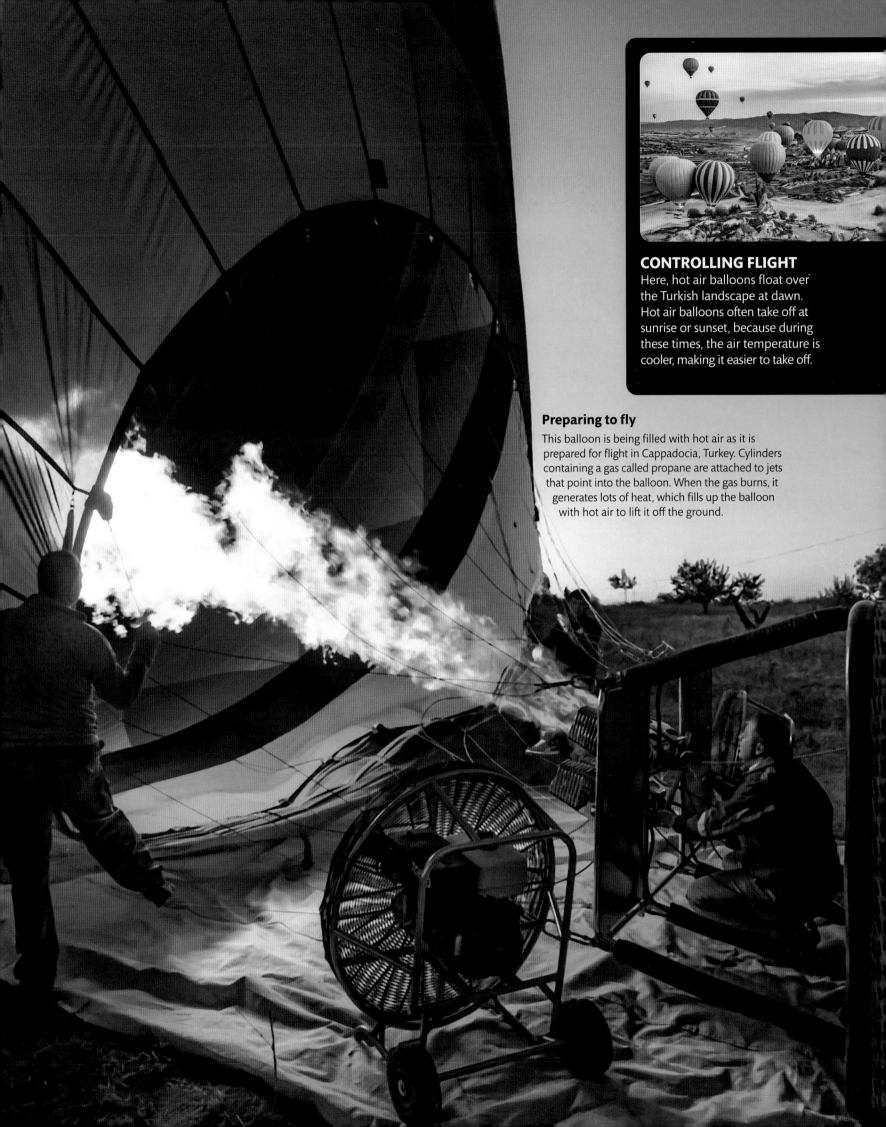

CONTROLLING FLIGHT
Here, hot air balloons float over the Turkish landscape at dawn. Hot air balloons often take off at sunrise or sunset, because during these times, the air temperature is cooler, making it easier to take off.

Preparing to fly
This balloon is being filled with hot air as it is prepared for flight in Cappadocia, Turkey. Cylinders containing a gas called propane are attached to jets that point into the balloon. When the gas burns, it generates lots of heat, which fills up the balloon with hot air to lift it off the ground.

Motors power the spinning propellers (the drone's rotors).

In 2020, drones delivered coronavirus tests to **2,500 clinics** in Rwanda and Ghana.

A part called the flight controller receives signals from the ground and controls the drone's movement.

A camera helps the person controlling the drone to see where it is going.

Large cargo of medical supplies

AERIAL ASSISTANTS
DRONES

Aerial vehicles called drones can take off, fly, or land anywhere without the need for a human pilot. When first designed, they were expensive military vehicles, but today drone technology is much more affordable and has been put to many uses. These include watering crops, monitoring rescue operations, and delivering essential supplies. One of the most widely used drones is the four-rotor quadcopter, which has four sets of propellers to lift it into the sky.

Medicine by air

Drones can be used to carry emergency medical packages, such as blood, organs, and personal protective equipment (PPE). Unlike ground-based vehicles, drones do not need roads or railways to reach their destinations. This makes them ideal for making deliveries in hard-to-reach places such as disaster zones.

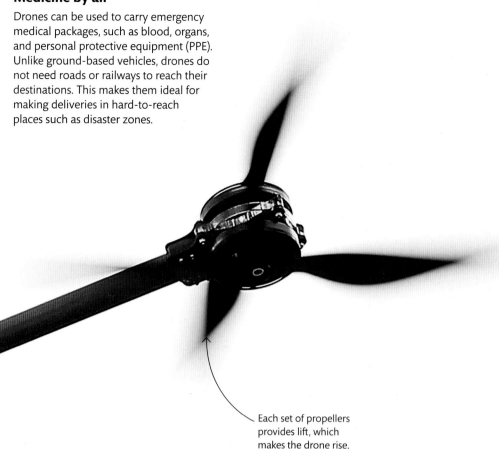

Each set of propellers provides lift, which makes the drone rise.

The frame provides a steady base for the drone to land on.

Fighting fires

Drones equipped with high-resolution cameras and other sensors can be used to track the spread of wildfires, helping firefighters plan how to tackle and extinguish the flames. Their small size enables them to reach places that are difficult for aircraft to get to.

Agricultural support

Farmers use drones for tasks such as sowing seeds, spraying fertilizers, or monitoring crop growth and health. The bird's-eye view from a drone can reveal issues that are not obvious from the ground and help farmers gather information over large areas.

Lighting up the sky

Drones equipped with lights can perform spectacular aerial displays. A group of them can be programmed with unique flight paths and other instructions, such as when to switch off and on. Each drone then forms part of a brightly lit, moving 3D image in the night sky.

FORCES OF FLIGHT

Four forces act on a flying machine—thrust and drag (or air resistance) act horizontally, while gravity and a force called lift act vertically. In a quadcopter drone, four spinning parts called rotors provide the lift and the thrust. When the drone's rotors produce enough lift to counteract gravity, the drone hovers. The drone's operator controls its flight by remotely adjusting the speed of its rotors.

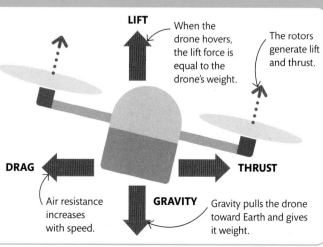

LIFT

When the drone hovers, the lift force is equal to the drone's weight.

The rotors generate lift and thrust.

DRAG

THRUST

Air resistance increases with speed.

GRAVITY

Gravity pulls the drone toward Earth and gives it weight.

SAVING SECONDS

WIND TUNNELS

A moving bicycle pushes air out of the way as it moves forward, but this becomes harder to do as its speed increases. The study of how air flows around an object, called aerodynamics, helps scientists find ways of making vehicles more streamlined so that they can pass through air more easily and quickly. They use wind tunnels to test the aerodynamics of bicycles, cars, aircraft, spacecraft, and sports equipment. In a wind tunnel, air is blown at vehicles through powerful fans and smoke is added to see how the air flows around it.

AIRCRAFT WINGS

Airplane designers use aerodynamics to design wings so that air flows faster above the wing than below it. That means that the air pressure is higher beneath the wing, resulting in an upward force, called lift, which enables aircraft to take off and remain airborne.

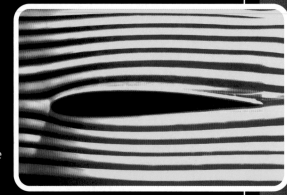

Va: 30,1 k
T: 22,3 °C
Beta: 0,0 Gr

AIR RESISTANCE

An object moving through air experiences air resistance, also known as drag. This is a force that acts against the object's direction of movement. Minimizing this resistance makes it easier for the object to speed up, or accelerate. When a cyclist leans forward, the curved shape of their body allows air to flow around them more easily. This reduces air resistance, making it easier for the cyclist to accelerate.

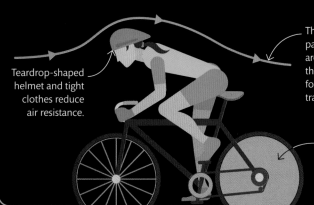

Teardrop-shaped helmet and tight clothes reduce air resistance.

The smoother the path of the air around the bike, the easier it is for the bike to travel through it.

Solid wheel allows air to flow around it more easily.

Built by NASA, the largest wind tunnel in the world is more than 1,400 ft (427 m) long.

Testing aerodynamics
A rider tests the aerodynamics of a bicycle at a Mercedes-Benz wind tunnel in Sindelfingen, Germany. Racing cyclists are eager to achieve high speeds, which means the bicycle's body needs to cut through air as easily as possible.

Protecting the crew

The Crew Module of the Orion spacecraft has a heat shield made of a material called AVCOAT, which disintegrates into hot plasma as it enters Earth's atmosphere. Underneath lies a carbon-fiber dome and a strong titanium structure that supports the body of the craft.

RETURNING TO EARTH

HEAT SHIELDS

Spacecraft reentering the atmosphere travel at incredibly high speeds. It takes energy to push through the air, and this is converted into heat. The temperature of the spacecraft can rise to as high as 5,000°F (2,800°C). To protect the astronauts inside, the spacecraft is designed with a special heat shield that disintegrates to form a hot gas called plasma, which carries away heat. The plasma is so hot that it glows with a bright yellow light.

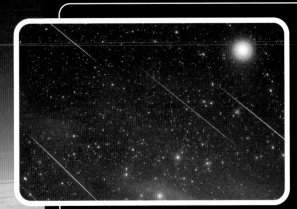

SHOOTING STARS

Meteors, or shooting stars, appear when chunks of rock from space enter Earth's atmosphere at high speed. Their passage through the air generates heat, which disintegrates the rocks, creating a streak of glowing plasma across the sky.

PLASMA

Plasma is made of gas atoms (see page 177) that are so energized that they lose their negatively charged electrons. They then form particles called ions, which have a positive charge. Plasma is found throughout the Universe, such as in flames, lightning bolts, and the surface of the Sun.

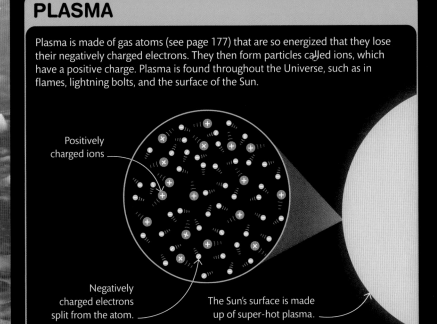

Positively charged ions

Negatively charged electrons split from the atom.

The Sun's surface is made up of super-hot plasma.

The Orion crew module can carry **4 astronauts** and everything they need to survive for up to 21 days.

SPACE MISSIONS
This Proton-M rocket carried two communications satellites into orbit on July 31, 2020. Rockets can also be used to transport astronauts and supplies to the International Space Station (ISS) and other planets and can even carry large parts of the ISS itself.

At launch, the rocket had a mass of **770 tons,** more than three-quarters of which was fuel.

SOARING INTO SPACE

ROCKETS

In order to escape Earth's atmosphere and enter orbit, a space rocket must reach speeds greater than 17,000 mph (25,000 km/h). The enormous force needed to accelerate a rocket to such speeds is provided by extremely powerful engines. These generate thrust by producing huge amounts of hot gas in extremely rapid chemical reactions. The thrust overcomes the force of the rocket's weight so that it can lift off into space.

SPEED DEMON

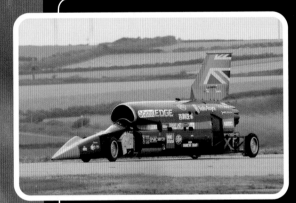

British car *Bloodhound* can accelerate to more than 630 mph (1,000 km/h) thanks to its huge jet engine. It is hoped it will one day break the land speed record. Jet engines are similar to rocket engines but burn fuel using oxygen from the air.

Blastoff

A Proton-M rocket lifts off from the Baikonur Cosmodrome in Russia. Extremely rapid chemical reactions between its fuel and another substance, called an oxidizer, produce expanding exhaust gases that push out through its nozzles.

UNBALANCED FORCES

Before a rocket launches, the forces acting on it are balanced—the upward force (produced by the launchpad) is equal to the downward force (the weight of the rocket). For it to take off, the rocket's thrust must be greater than the rocket's weight.

The thrust of the engines is greater than the rocket's weight, so it accelerates the rocket upward.

THRUST

The weight of the rocket is reduced as fuel is used up.

WEIGHT

The weight of the rocket pushes down on the launchpad.

The launchpad's surface produces an upward force called a reaction.

WEIGHT

REACTION

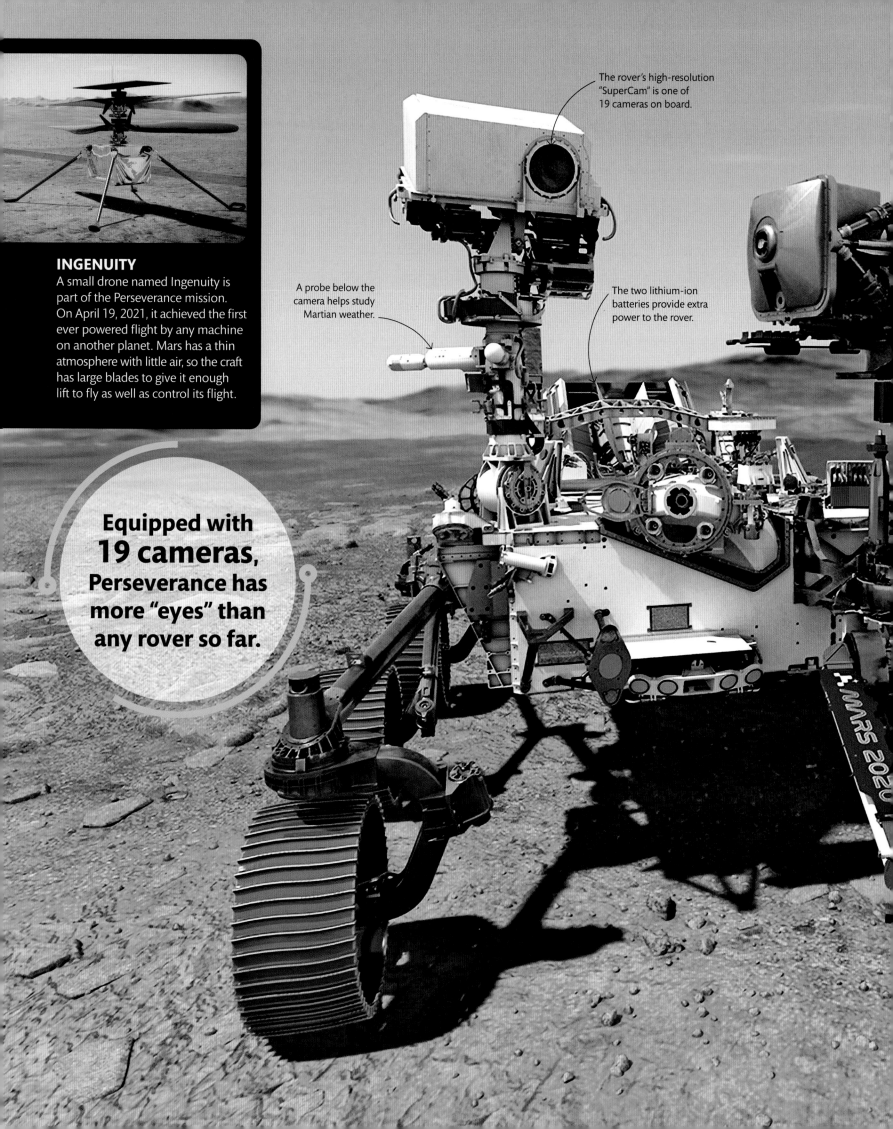

INGENUITY

A small drone named Ingenuity is part of the Perseverance mission. On April 19, 2021, it achieved the first ever powered flight by any machine on another planet. Mars has a thin atmosphere with little air, so the craft has large blades to give it enough lift to fly as well as control its flight.

The rover's high-resolution "SuperCam" is one of 19 cameras on board.

A probe below the camera helps study Martian weather.

The two lithium-ion batteries provide extra power to the rover.

Equipped with 19 cameras, Perseverance has more "eyes" than any rover so far.

MARS 2020

Surveying Mars

Perseverance landed on Mars inside the Jezero Crater, believed to be a former lake. Its landing site is thought to have been an ancient river delta, which may contain signs of past life. The rover analyzes the area using its several high-tech but lightweight gadgets and sensors.

The robotic arm has a drill that helps the rover extract rock core samples for study, which will be returned to Earth in the future.

EXPLORING SPACE

PERSEVERANCE ROVER

Humans explore the Solar System to understand Earth and its place in the Universe. We have walked on our Moon and sent probes to explore the planets in our Solar System. The robotic rover Perseverance, which launched into space in 2020 and landed on the surface of Mars in 2021, can communicate with Earth using radio signals. Its main tasks are to conduct scientific experiments, gather rock samples that can be sent to Earth for study, and hunt for signs of ancient microscopic life

THE SOLAR SYSTEM

In our Solar System, there are eight planets traveling around a star, the Sun. The planets move around the Sun in elliptical paths called orbits. The fourth planet from the Sun, Mars is one of Earth's closest neighbors, 34 million miles (55 million km) away at its nearest point, so we can travel to it in only a few months.

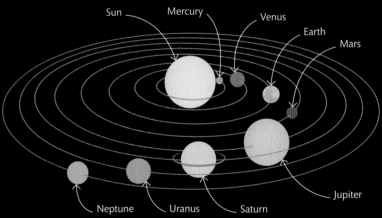

Sun Mercury Venus Earth Mars Jupiter Saturn Uranus Neptune

Mars

Famously known as the Red Planet, Mars gets its dusty orange colour from the high levels of iron oxide—the substance that gives rust its colour—on its surface. Plenty of ice has been discovered on Mars that indicates that it was once warmer, wetter, and had a thicker atmosphere—ideal for life. This has spurred scientists to search for signs of microscopic life.

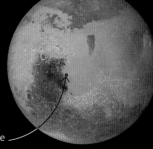

Perseverance landing site

SOS SIGNALS

FLARES

During an emergency at sea or on a mountain, it is important for rescuers to be able to locate those in danger as quickly as possible. One way to signal for help is by using flares. These contain chemicals that burn with a bright, colored flame that can be seen from miles away, pinpointing where the rescuers need to go. They can come in different colors, which are produced by different chemicals, but most are a deep red. Flares can be used both during the day and at night. Some flares emit thick smoke instead of light. These are used in places where the ground is not clearly visible from the sky, such as forests.

GUNPOWDER

Flares contain a chemical that releases oxygen when heated, making the flare burn brightly. Gunpowder also contains this chemical, along with sulfur and charcoal. While flares are designed to burn safely, gunpowder is tightly packed to explode.

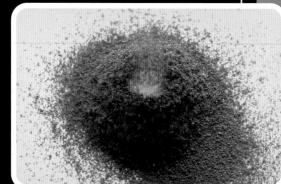

FLAME TESTS

When put into a hot flame, different metal salts cause the flame to change color. Scientists can use these "flame tests" to work out which metal is present in a particular salt. A wire loop dipped in a small amount of the salt is placed in a blue Bunsen flame, and the color is observed. Bright red means strontium is present, while calcium gives orange and sodium gives yellow flames.

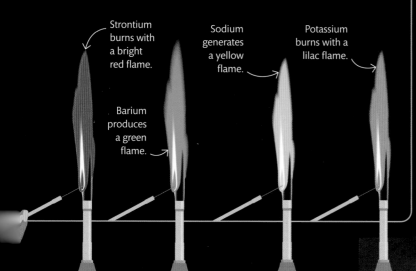

Strontium burns with a bright red flame.

Barium produces a green flame.

Sodium generates a yellow flame.

Potassium burns with a lilac flame.

Handheld flares can burn for about **1 minute** and can be seen up to **3 miles** (5 km) away.

Calling for help

On the icy slopes of Fairfield, UK, a rescue helicopter is being guided to the site of an accident by a flare burning with a bright red flame. Flares are also very effective during rescues at sea, especially at night.

The fireworks display at the Celebration of Light in Vancouver, Canada, fills the night sky with brilliant colors. The different colors are produced when different metals are heated as the fireworks burn—barium for green and magnesium for white.

Into the sky

A catapult officer, or "shooter," aboard the USS *Theodore Roosevelt* gives a clear signal to the pilot of a F/A-18F Super Hornet after checking the wind speed and direction. Just below the deck lies the steam catapult needed to help launch the plane into the air.

The F/A-18F Super Hornet is more than **60 ft (18 m)** long and is used by the US military.

SKYWARD BOOST
AIRCRAFT CATAPULTS

An airplane normally requires a long runway to gain the speed required for takeoff. This is not possible when taking off from ships at sea, so the decks of aircraft carriers are equipped with powerful catapult systems that drag the planes along, helping them go from 0 to 150 mph (a standing start to 250 km/h) in just two seconds. Most aircraft carrier catapults are powered by the pressure exerted by superheated steam.

STEAM PRESSURE

The amount by which a force is concentrated or spread out is called pressure. The pressure to power an aircraft catapult is created by heating water. This turns it into steam (a gas) and causes its molecules to move very fast. These fast-moving molecules exert a force on the container they are in, pushing on the piston.

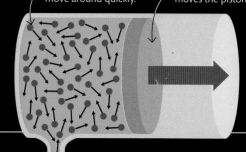

Steam molecules move around quickly.

The pressure moves the piston.

SLINGSHOTS

Slingshots, also known as catapults, work in a different way from the catapults aboard aircraft carriers. Pulling back on the rubber band of a slingshot stores energy in it. That energy then propels a stone or other object forward when the rubber band is released.

How steam catapults work

Just before takeoff, hot steam held in a large accumulator tank is released through pipes into the main cylinder that runs along the length of the runway, just below the deck. The steam's pressure pushes a piston that drags along a shuttle with enormous force—pulling the plane forward at great speed.

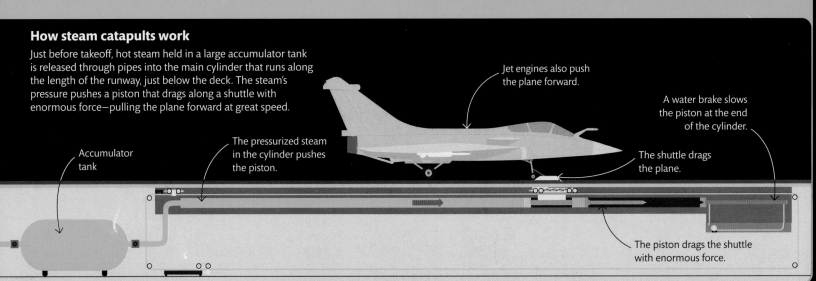

Jet engines also push the plane forward.

A water brake slows the piston at the end of the cylinder.

Accumulator tank

The pressurized steam in the cylinder pushes the piston.

The shuttle drags the plane.

The piston drags the shuttle with enormous force.

DELIVERING DATA

FIBER-OPTIC CABLES

Every day, vast amounts of data are sent around the globe safely and quickly using fiber-optic cables. These cables contain strands of glass, called optical fibers, that are as thin as a hair. Data speeds through these fibers as pulses of light, reflecting back and forth between their walls as it races from continent to continent. Today, the internet, television, and telephone systems all rely on fiber-optic cable networks.

INSIDE A CABLE

A fiber-optic cable contains optical fibers, individually wrapped in a layer called cladding. The fibers are then bundled together and sealed in a tube to protect the cables when they are laid out in exposed environments, such as the seabed.

LIGHT AND REFLECTION

In optical fibers, information is carried in light signals. Light is transferred through the fibers by a process called total internal reflection, as it travels in a zigzag pattern. The light wave bounces from one side of the cable to the other but never hits the edge of the glass at an angle steep enough to pass through, so it is always completely reflected—all the way through the length of the cable.

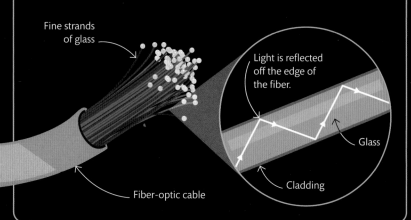

Fine strands of glass

Light is reflected off the edge of the fiber.

Glass

Cladding

Fiber-optic cable

1 Winding up the cable
Undersea cables are laid using specialized ships and other machinery. First, the fiber-optic cable, which can be hundreds of miles long, is coiled up on board the ship in preparation for the voyage.

The fastest fiber-optic cables can carry **30 million** phone calls at once.

2 Off to sea
The ship travels to the right location, where the cable is connected to a point on land. The ship then starts to move, rolling out the cable behind it as it goes.

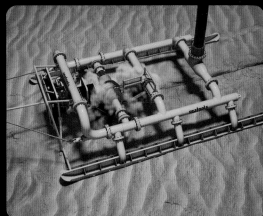

3 Settling into the seabed
Once on the seabed, the cable is fed out through a plow. As the plow is dragged after the ship and carves out a trench in the seabed, the cable is safely buried.

4 Maintaining **the cable**
Despite many measures to protect undersea cables, they can be damaged. Mending them requires divers or small submarines to investigate, then bring the affected section to the surface for repair.

Avalanche alerts

Mountaineers in avalanche-prone areas, such as this team in the Swiss Alps, have to carry radio transceivers as part of their emergency kit. These devices continuously send out radio signals. If someone goes missing, others set their devices to receive radio signals, allowing them to pick up signals from the missing person's device. People who have been trapped by falling snow from an avalanche can then be safely located and rescued.

EMERGENCY RESCUE

RADIO COMMUNICATION

Long-distance communication was slow and difficul for centuries before the discovery of radio waves made wireless communication possible. Radio waves are a type of electromagnetic radiation (see page 142) that can be used to send signals over large distances at great speed Many modern communication methods involve a device called a transceiver, which contains antennas that can both send and receive radio waves, acting as a transmitter as wel as a receiver. Radio communication is used in mobile phones, radio, radar, Wi-Fi, and other applications

GOING KEYLESS
A smart key fob is a small electronic device that allows access to a vehicle without using a regular key. When triggered, a transmitter sends a radio signal to a receiver that locks or unlocks the door.

RADIO SIGNALS

Radio waves have the longest wavelengths in the electromagnetic spectrum, which enable them to travel far. They are generated by a transmitter using changing electric currents. By adding a signal to a radio wave, information can be encoded in the wave, which is then radiated outward from antennas. A receiver works like a transmitter in reverse, receiving the waves and turning them back into electric currents.

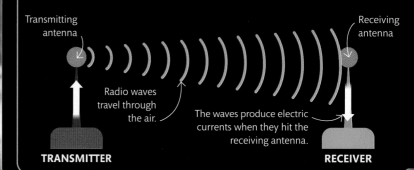

Transmitting antenna

Receiving antenna

Radio waves travel through the air.

The waves produce electric currents when they hit the receiving antenna.

TRANSMITTER

RECEIVER

Many **objects** in **space**, such as the Sun and other large stars, **emit** radio waves.

IDENTITY CHECKS

BIOMETRICS

Every day, people access their mobile phones or tablets using biometrics—body measurements. Each person has many unique physical and behavioral characteristics, such as their fingerprints, facial features, tone of voice, or even the pattern of a part of their eye called the iris. Biometrics uses these traits to digitally identify a person by checking them against a database containing information about the features of many users. This technology is used by companies to verify employees and by the police.

This image shows iris details as a sequence of light and dark patches, which are converted into digital data to be checked against a database.

THE HUMAN EYE

Our eyes turn reflected light into the images we see. Incoming light passes through the lens of the eye and focuses on the retina at the back. This produces electrical signals that are sent to the brain, which then works out what we are seeing.

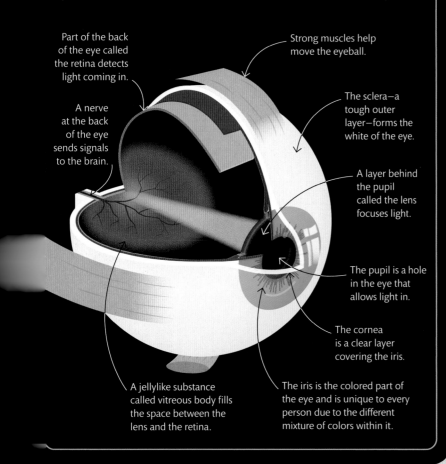

Part of the back of the eye called the retina detects light coming in.

A nerve at the back of the eye sends signals to the brain.

Strong muscles help move the eyeball.

The sclera—a tough outer layer—forms the white of the eye.

A layer behind the pupil called the lens focuses light.

The pupil is a hole in the eye that allows light in.

The cornea is a clear layer covering the iris.

A jellylike substance called vitreous body fills the space between the lens and the retina.

The iris is the colored part of the eye and is unique to every person due to the different mixture of colors within it.

The iris scanner analyzes the iris by dividing it into eight sections.

Iris scan

The colored part of the eye called the iris is scanned in this computer image. The different colors in the iris create a pattern unique to each individual, which can be used to accurately identify them.

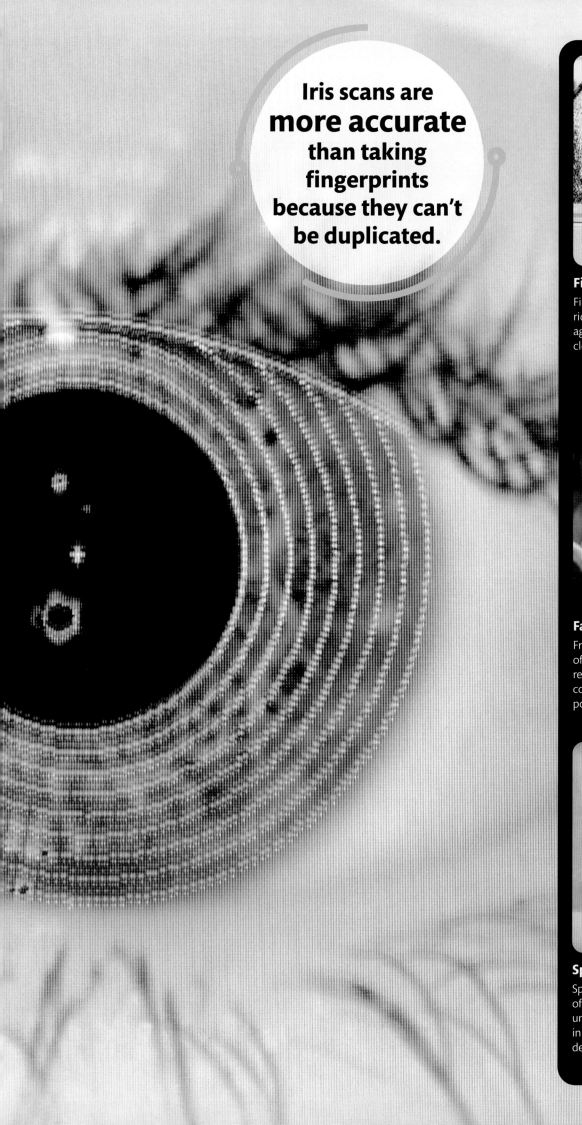

Iris scans are **more accurate** than taking fingerprints because they can't be duplicated.

Fingerprint scan

Fingerprint scanners work by capturing the pattern of ridges and valleys on a finger. The data is compared against a database of other fingerprints to find the closest match and identify the individual.

Facial recognition

From the distance between the eyes to the length of the jawline, every face has unique features. Facial recognition systems take these measurements and compare them against a database of face shapes. A positive match confirms the identity of the person.

Speech recognition

Speech recognition systems compare the sounds of our voice against a database of word sounds to understand how we normally sound when using words in a sentence. This allows the user to command smart devices to carry out certain tasks by speaking to them.

Global gaming

Players of popular game *Fortnite* attend the ESL Katowice Royale competition in Poland in 2019. Tournaments like these are massive events that attract teams, spectators, and sponsors from all over the world and are livestreamed on the internet.

In 2021, the highest-earning eSports team, Team Liquid, had won **$36 million** in prize money.

PLAYING TOGETHER

ONLINE GAMING

The internet has changed the way we learn, work, and even play—enabling us to create huge video game tournaments where elite players and teams compete in the same game environment simultaneously. The internet can connect far-flung game servers, or just many computers in a single place through a local area network. Everything connected to the internet uses a set of rules to transfer data, enabling remote communication.

THE INTERNET OF THINGS
Billions of devices share data over the internet, and this interconnected system is nicknamed the internet of things. This encompasses everything that connects to the internet, such as smart watches, driverless cars, and air quality monitors.

THE INTERNET

The internet is the worldwide system of connected computer networks—joined together by infrastructure such as satellites and cables (see page 112). Home devices such as computers access the internet via an internet service provider (ISP).

WI-FI ROUTER ((•)) 1. Devices connect to a router.   **LOCAL AREA NETWORK**

2. They can also connect to others nearby through a local area network (LAN).

3. Data is sent through the telephone exchange.   4. Through an ISP, computers can access the internet.

CORE ROUTER

TELEPHONE EXCHANGE   **INTERNET SERVICE PROVIDER**   5. The core router connects to all of the internet.

PROTECTING AND SURVIVING

Earth is the only planet we know that has life on it, and this miracle of life is precious and fragile. Science has enabled us to create medicine to treat diseases and infections, machines to keep us alive, and prosthetics to help us move. Scientific innovations can also help reduce the effects of climate change and conserve the natural environment around us.

DEFEATING DISEASES

ANTIBIOTICS

Bacteria are tiny organisms that can cause diseases such as pneumonia. However, some bacteria and fungi (another type of organism) naturally produce substances to fight off and kill competing bacteria. Scientists use these to create antibiotics, which work as medicine to treat diseases that result from bacterial infections. More than half of the antibiotics in use today come from different species of the bacteria called *Streptomyces*, which can grow in large colonies.

ANTIBIOTIC RESISTANCE
Bacteria that are in contact with antibiotics for too long can evolve the ability to resist them. Antibiotic-resistant bacteria, such as methicillin-resistant *Staphylococcus aureus* (MRSA) seen here, can cause dangerous infections that cannot be treated.

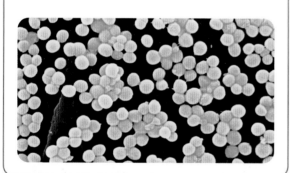

BACTERIA
Bacteria are single-celled organisms and are the most common living things. Most bacteria are helpful. Around 40 trillion of them live in your body, and the bacteria in your gut help you digest food. Some types are harmful and can cause infection. Antibiotics work in different ways to kill bacteria or prevent them from working.

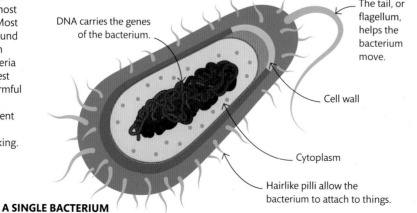

DNA carries the genes of the bacterium.

The tail, or flagellum, helps the bacterium move.

Cell wall

Cytoplasm

Hairlike pilli allow the bacterium to attach to things.

A SINGLE BACTERIUM

These droplets are used to make the antibiotic.

Less than 1 percent of all bacteria species on Earth cause disease.

Lab-grown colony of *Streptomyces* bacteria

Bacterial colony

A colony of *Streptomyces coelicolor* bacteria is seen here in a magnified image. These bacteria release fluid droplets, which help scientists make as many as five different antibiotics. These are then taken in the form of tablets.

Bacteria killer
This spot of mold is a growing clump of the fungus *Penicillium*. The chemicals inside the fungus are killing the surrounding spots of red bacteria, causing them to lose their color. *Penicillium* was originally used to make the lifesaving antibiotic penicillin.

COMBATING COVID-19

VACCINES

In 2020, a pandemic swept across the globe. It was caused by a harmful microorganism—an organism so small, it can only be seen with a microscope—called a virus. This virus, known as a coronavirus, infected people's lungs and caused a disease called COVID-19. To stop healthy people from catching the virus, scientists developed vaccines. These are medicines that teach the body to identify and fight off the virus. There are similar vaccines for a wide range of diseases.

VIRUS VARIATIONS

Viruses keep changing their structure, giving rise to different versions of the same virus called variants. This is why every year a flu vaccine is developed to combat the latest variant infecting people. Every vaccine is tested on volunteers to ensure it is safe and effective.

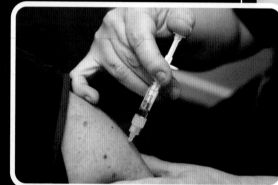

The virus has spikes on its surface that make it distinctive to the immune system.

HOW VACCINES WORK

Vaccines make use of the body's system for fighting off disease, called the immune system. Part of the immune system learns to identify pathogens (harmful viruses or bacteria) that enter the body so that the body can destroy them quickly if they enter it again at a later time. It does this by producing substances called antibodies, which mark the pathogens for destruction whenever they appear. Vaccines cause the immune system to produce antibodies for a specific pathogen without the pathogen being present. This means the body will be protected against a disease without having to be exposed to it first.

Antibodies produced by the immune system

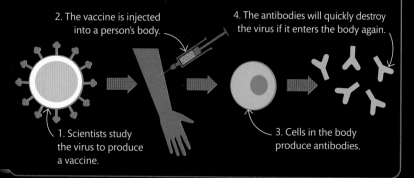

2. The vaccine is injected into a person's body.

4. The antibodies will quickly destroy the virus if it enters the body again.

1. Scientists study the virus to produce a vaccine.

3. Cells in the body produce antibodies.

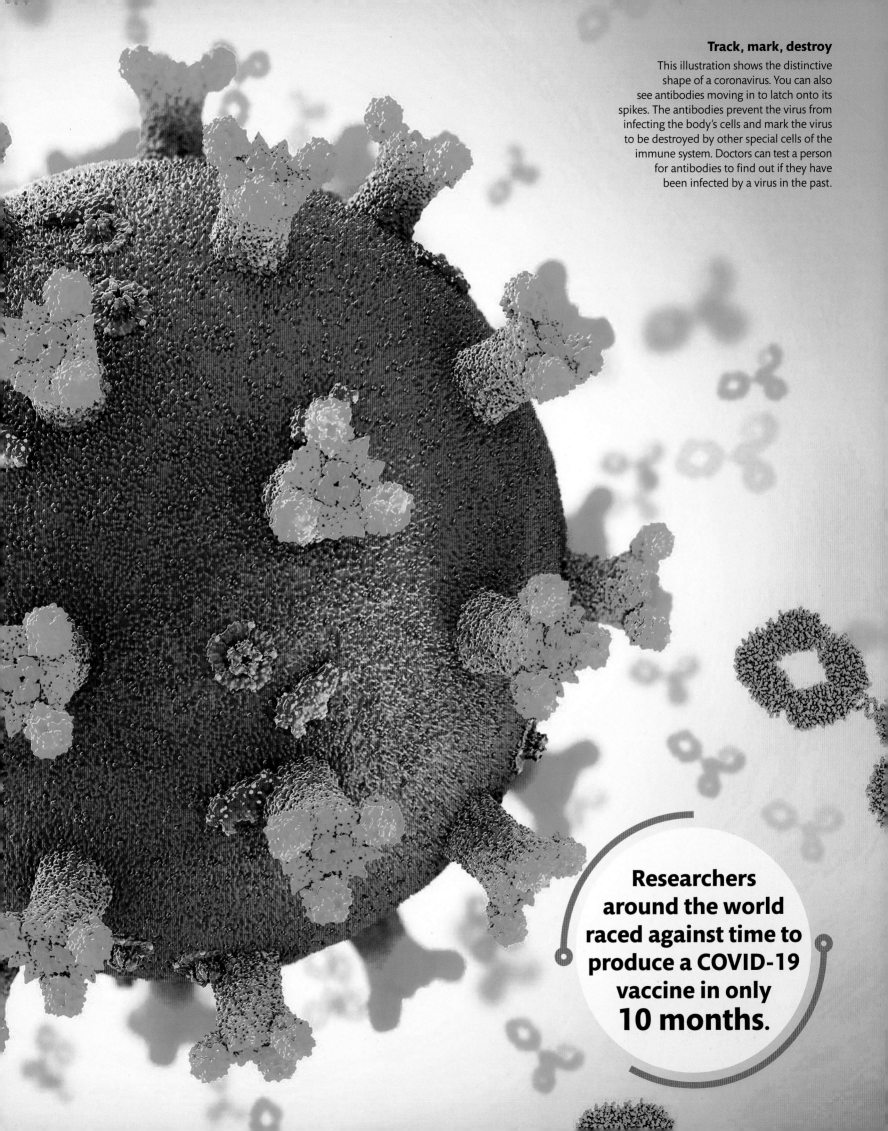

Track, mark, destroy
This illustration shows the distinctive shape of a coronavirus. You can also see antibodies moving in to latch onto its spikes. The antibodies prevent the virus from infecting the body's cells and mark the virus to be destroyed by other special cells of the immune system. Doctors can test a person for antibodies to find out if they have been infected by a virus in the past.

Researchers around the world raced against time to produce a COVID-19 vaccine in only 10 months.

LIFE-GIVING LIQUID

BLOOD DONATION

Like skin and bone, blood is a tissue—a collection of specialized cells. Blood carries oxygen and carbon dioxide around the body, transports other important nutrients, and helps keep our bodies at the right temperature. It also contains white blood cells, which fight off infections and produce antibodies to protect us (see page 122). If blood is lost during surgery, or more is needed to treat a medical condition, it can be provided by a blood donor.

BLOOD TESTS

Blood tests are an important part of medicine. They are used to measure the amount of substances in the body, such as salts, fats, and sugars. The results tell doctors how well a person's kidneys, liver, and other organs are working.

BLOOD

Blood is made up of different kinds of cell floating in a watery liquid called plasma. Pumped by the heart, it travels around the human body in tiny tubes called blood vessels. There are three types of cells—red, white, and platelets—and each one does a different job.

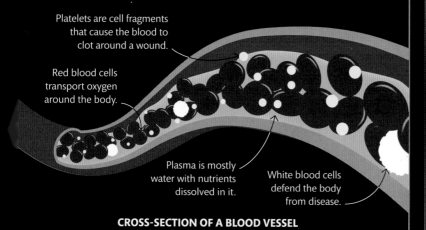

Platelets are cell fragments that cause the blood to clot around a wound.

Red blood cells transport oxygen around the body.

Plasma is mostly water with nutrients dissolved in it.

White blood cells defend the body from disease.

CROSS-SECTION OF A BLOOD VESSEL

Donating blood

Blood is essential for the healthy working of the human body. If blood is lost, a person's life can be saved by giving them a blood transfusion—pumping someone else's blood into their body. This is made possible by volunteers donating blood, which is then sent to hospitals where it is needed. Over time, the donor's body is able to replace the blood given.

Blood makes up about 8 percent of the weight of an adult human's body.

BLOOD BAGS
There are four main blood groups: A, B, AB, and O. Receiving the wrong type can be life-threatening due to the differences between them. However, people with what is called O negative blood are universal donors. In an emergency, their blood can be safely given to anyone.

HELPING THE HEART BEAT

PACEMAKERS

The pacemaker is a lifesaving invention that helps control the human heartbeat. Millions of people around the world suffer from some form of irregular heartbeat, which can lead to health problems. A pacemaker is a small, battery-powered device that sits inside the body and senses the heartbeat, correcting it when it goes out of rhythm by creating tiny pulses of electricity.

The battery in a pacemaker can last for about **10 years.**

TINY TECH

Pacemakers need to be very small to avoid interfering with the body, so most are around the size of a matchbox. Scientists are developing even smaller ones, some as tiny as a pill.

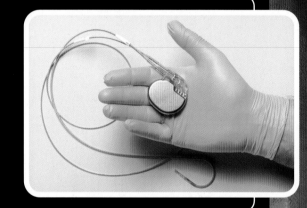

THE HEART

The heart is a powerful organ that pumps blood through the body by contracting and relaxing in a rhythm controlled by electrical signals. The heart has two sides, each containing two chambers—an atrium and a ventricle. As the heart beats, it sends blood to the lungs, where it picks up oxygen. The heart then sucks this blood back, and pumps it out to the rest of the body.

5. A large tube called the aorta carries oxygen-rich blood to the body.

3. Oxygen-rich blood enters the heart from the lungs.

1. Oxygen-poor blood from the body arrives in the right atrium.

2. The right ventricle pushes blood out to the lungs.

4. The left ventricle pushes oxygen-rich blood out of the heart.

▶ **OXYGEN-POOR BLOOD**
▷ **OXYGEN-RICH BLOOD**

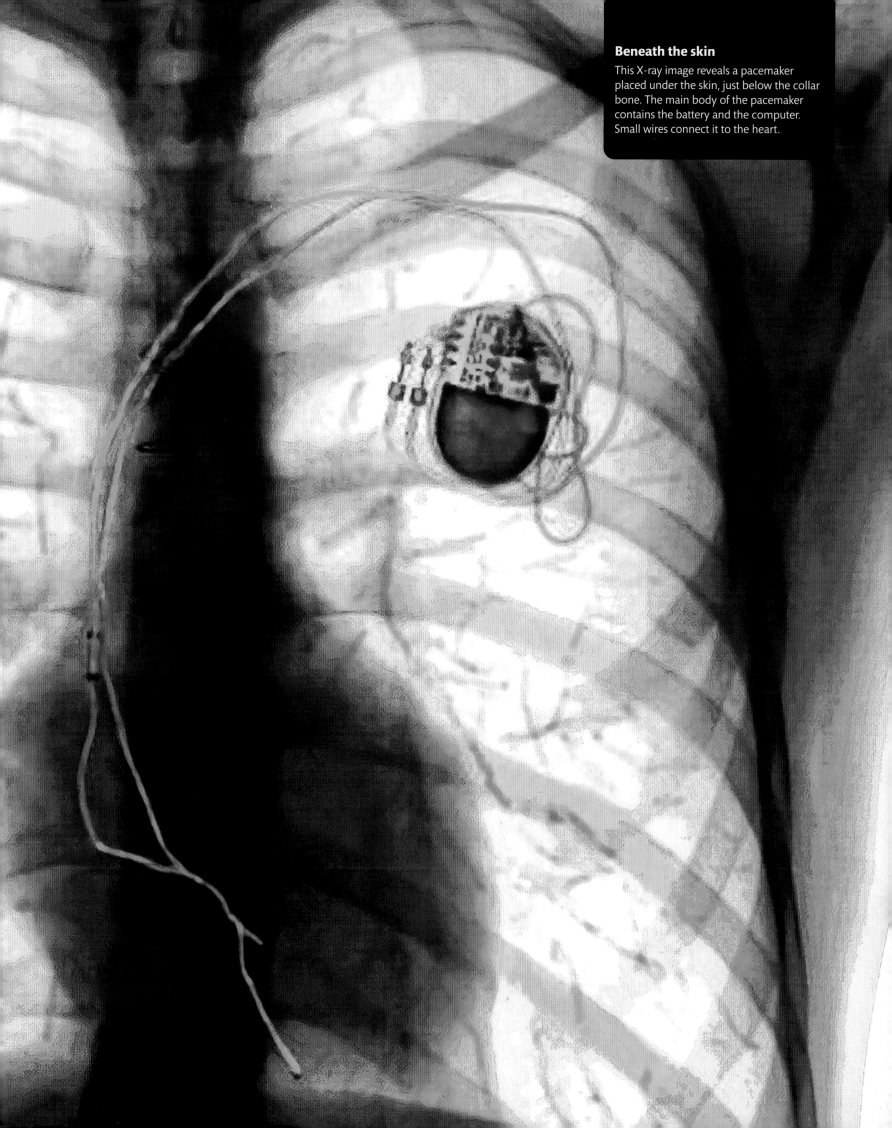

Beneath the skin
This X-ray image reveals a pacemaker placed under the skin, just below the collar bone. The main body of the pacemaker contains the battery and the computer. Small wires connect it to the heart.

EXTRA STRENGTH
Some exoskeletons are designed to enhance human abilities. Several models have been trialed in the military to enable soldiers to carry heavy loads over long distances without overexerting their own muscles.

MOBILITY MACHINE

EXOSKELETONS

In nature, exoskeletons are armorlike structures that support the bodies of animals such as insects. Artificial human-made exoskeletons work similarly—they are wearable machines that support and enhance how the body moves using a system of sensors, motors, levers, and other parts. Some exoskeletons can sense the signals sent by the body's nervous system and interpret these, while others work using sensors in the shoes that activate when a person's body weight shifts.

One step at a time

At the Cyberdyne facility in Nordrhein-Westfalen, Germany, people with damage to their lower nervous systems are using the HAL exoskeleton to help them regain mobility. The exoskeleton supports the movements of the patient's limbs and then feeds back to the brain, strengthening the connection between the brain and the limb.

In 2020, American Adam Gorlitsky ran a **33-hour marathon** while wearing a type of exoskeleton.

THE NERVOUS SYSTEM

1. The brain is the body's control center, processing information and responding.

The nervous system controls the body's activity. When the human body senses changes in its surroundings, nerve cells send signals to the brain, which decides how to respond. It then sends information in the form of electrical signals to other parts of the body, such as to the muscles to control movement.

2. The spinal cord carries electrical signals from the brain to the rest of the body.

3. A network of nerves runs throughout the body.

The brain sends signals to the muscles in the leg via the spinal cord.

How exoskeletons work

One type of exoskeleton, called the HAL, works by using electrical sensors placed on the skin to detect the signals sent from the brain to various muscles. These signals are picked up and sent to the exoskeleton's control system, which moves the appropriate part of the suit to help that part of the body move.

The sensors detect electrical signals in muscles associated with movement.

The control system uses sensor information to move the exoskeleton.

SUPPORT SYSTEMS

MEDICAL MACHINES

Human bodies are made up of complicated systems that can sometimes break down. Over the last century, remarkable technological achievements have meant that machines can sometimes step in and provide critical assistance to whichever system in the body is failing. While some machines are used to better understand how the body works, others detect problems, and others fix them.

HUMAN BODY SYSTEMS

Inside our bodies are many systems of connected organs and tissues, all specialized to carry out different important jobs. Our digestive system enables us to eat and gain energy from food, our respiratory system allows us to breathe, and our circulatory system keeps our blood flowing around our body.

The lungs are part of the respiratory system and take oxygen from the air and pass it to the blood.

The brain is the control center of the nervous system, which coordinates how the body responds to things.

Blood vessels make up the circulatory system, as the heart (see page 130) pumps blood around the body.

The bladder is part of the urinary system, which gets rid of the body's waste.

The small and large intestines process food and are part of the digestive system.

Hard bones keep the body upright and work together with the muscles.

Along with bones, muscles make up the musculoskeletal system, which makes your body move, as muscles pull on the bones of the skeleton.

Understanding the brain

An electroencephalogram (or EEG) allows scientists to study how the brain works. The small disks attached to the woman's head are electrodes, which measure the electrical pulses of brain activity.

Scientists use EEGs to study brain activity during dreams and sleep.

Defibrillator

If the heart—the center of our circulatory system—stops beating, or its beat becomes irregular, then first aiders only have moments to act. Defibrillators can send bursts of electricity into the heart to get it beating regularly again.

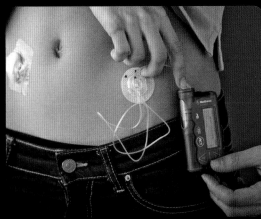

Insulin pump

Insulin is usually released by the pancreas and is important for balancing the amount of sugar in the blood. People with a condition called diabetes can't produce enough insulin naturally but can use an insulin pump to top up their levels.

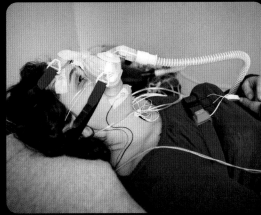

CPAP machines

Some people have trouble with their respiratory system, especially while sleeping, and can't get enough air. Continuous positive airway pressure (CPAP) machines use mild pressure to keep air going in and out of the lungs so that patients can breathe.

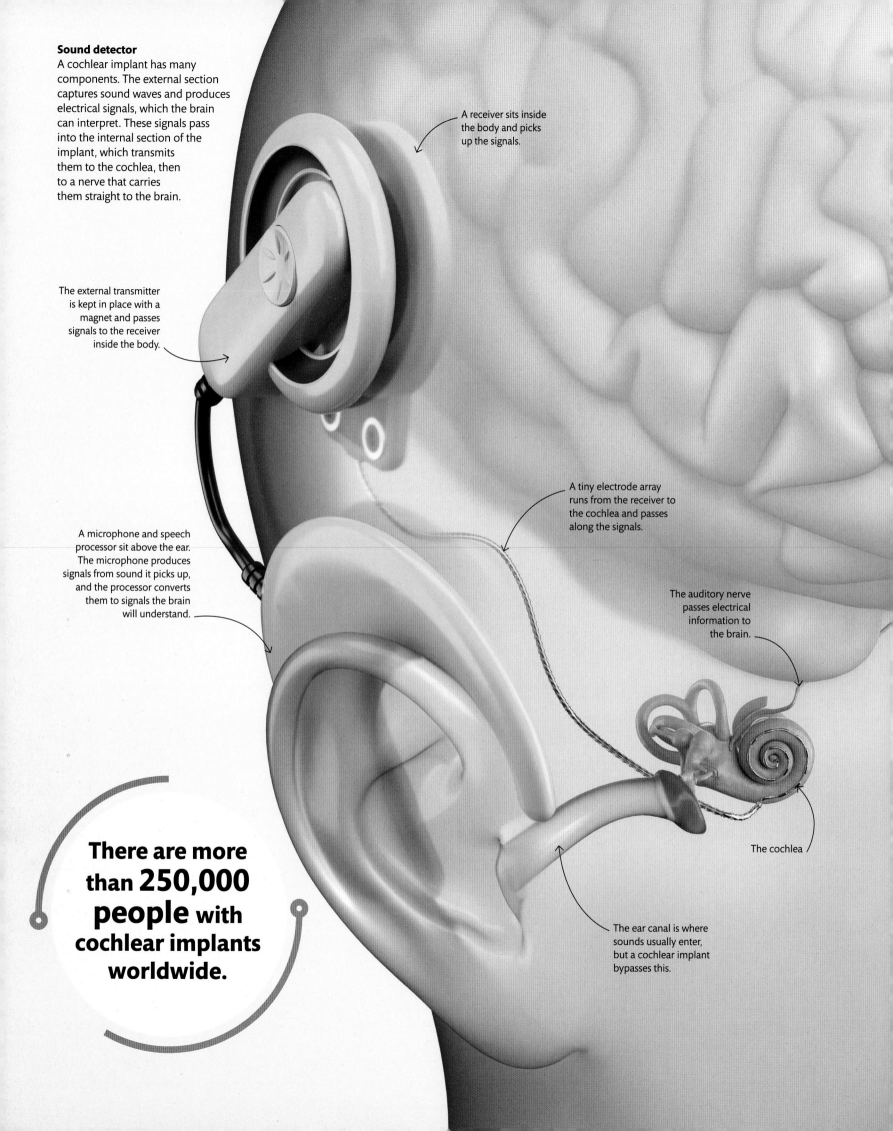

Sound detector
A cochlear implant has many components. The external section captures sound waves and produces electrical signals, which the brain can interpret. These signals pass into the internal section of the implant, which transmits them to the cochlea, then to a nerve that carries them straight to the brain.

A receiver sits inside the body and picks up the signals.

The external transmitter is kept in place with a magnet and passes signals to the receiver inside the body.

A microphone and speech processor sit above the ear. The microphone produces signals from sound it picks up, and the processor converts them to signals the brain will understand.

A tiny electrode array runs from the receiver to the cochlea and passes along the signals.

The auditory nerve passes electrical information to the brain.

The cochlea

The ear canal is where sounds usually enter, but a cochlear implant bypasses this.

There are more than 250,000 people with cochlear implants worldwide.

SENSING SOUNDS

COCHLEAR IMPLANTS

Hearing aids can help people who cannot hear well by amplifying the sounds in their ear. However, some people have such profound hearing loss that this doesn't work. Cochlear implants are an invention designed to bypass the inner ear by converting sound into electrical signals, which are then transmitted directly into the brain. One part is surgically implanted and the other sits outside the body on the side of the head.

The brain receives the signals and processes them.

SEEING BY SENSORS

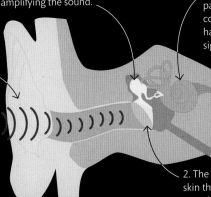

Bionic eyes work in a similar way to cochlear implants and are designed to help people with sight loss, although they are not yet widely available. They use a camera mounted on glasses to pick up visual information and send it directly to the brain.

THE EAR

Hearing is simply our ear and brain interpreting vibrations in the air. When sound waves reach our ear, they make the eardrum vibrate. These vibrations travel through tiny bones to the cochlea, which converts them into signals for the brain.

3. The vibrations move tiny bones in the middle ear, amplifying the sound.

1. The outer ear collects sound waves and funnels them into the ear.

4. Waves of sound pass into the cochlea, moving tiny hair cells, which pass signals to the brain.

2. The eardrum is a thin skin that vibrates when sound waves hit it.

Running blades are made of several layers of **carbon fiber**—each layer thinner than a human hair.

WR   PR

PARALYMPIC SPORT
RUNNING BLADES

Artificial lower limbs worn by amputee athletes are called running blades. Rather than copying biological legs, they are designed to be light, curved, and elastic, which means that they return to their original size and shape after being deformed by a force. They behave like leg muscles and tendons—under the wearer's weight, they bend and store energy, then release it as they push off the ground.

EXTRA BOUNCE

The bouncing boost of a trampoline comes from the springs that attach the fabric "bed" to the rigid frame. When a person jumps, their weight forces the springs to extend downward. The springs exert an equal and opposite (upward) force on the person as they return to their original position—sending the person bouncing up into the air.

ELASTICITY

A running blade functions like a spring. When an athlete takes a stride, they apply a force to the blade that causes it to bend, storing a type of energy called elastic potential energy (see page 42). The elastic blade unbends as it returns to its original shape, exerting force and releasing the stored energy. This energy changes to kinetic energy that pushes the athlete forward.

Blade pushed downward

Blade pushes forward

1. The weight of the user bends the blade, storing potential energy inside it.

2. The weight is shifted to the tip of the blade, preparing the user.

3. The blade bounces back, providing force, and the user is pushed forward.

CRASH TESTING

To determine how safe a new vehicle is, engineers conduct crash tests that mimic what happens in real-life accidents. During a collision, a moving car comes to a sudden stop, but its passengers have the same momentum as before and continue moving, which can result in injury. By collecting data, crash tests help minimize the risk of injury and improve the safety features of a vehicle, such as airbags and seatbelts.

way people move on impact. Each dummy contains more than 130 sensors that record the chances of injury during different crash scenarios, providing data to improve car safety.

During a crash test, vehicles crash at an average speed of **35 mph** (56 km/h).

MOMENTUM

Momentum is a measure of how much movement an object has. The faster an object moves, and the more mass it has, the greater its momentum. When a car crashes, its momentum changes quickly, but the passengers keep moving, which puts them in danger. Airbags and seatbelts safely change passengers' momentum, and crumple zones slow the change in the car's momentum.

Airbags safely reduce the momentum of the dummy's head, helping reduce injury.

A crumple zone at each end of the car absorbs much of the impact during a collision, slowing the car's change in momentum.

Crash test dummy

A seatbelt stretches to slow down the movement of the dummy on impact.

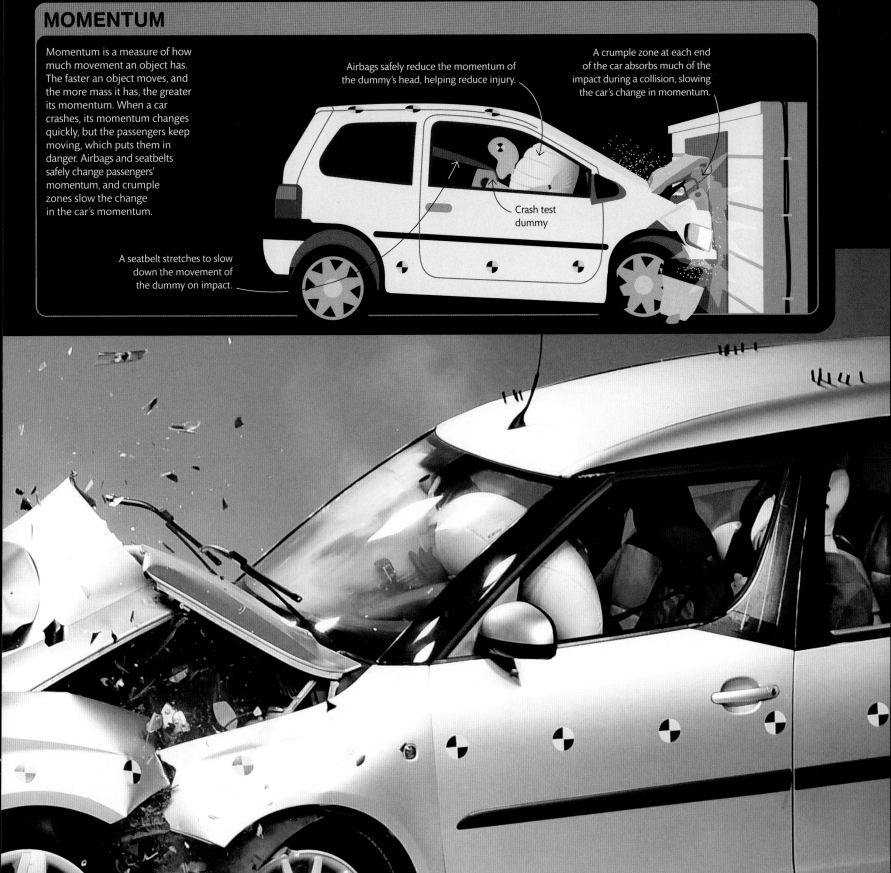

Simulating accidents

Vehicles collide at a motor racing track near Paris, France. This test was carried out without using seatbelts in the backseat and was designed to show why seatbelts are essential and encourage car manufacturers to improve the safety of their design.

STERILIZING WITH LIGHT

UV RADIATION

The light we see all around us is a form of energy called electromagnetic radiation. All radiation travels in waves, and most of these waves are too long or short to be seen by the human eye, such as ultraviolet (UV). UV is naturally produced by the Sun and other stars, but it can also be created on Earth using special lamps. These lamps have many uses, including disinfecting surfaces and revealing evidence in forensic investigations.

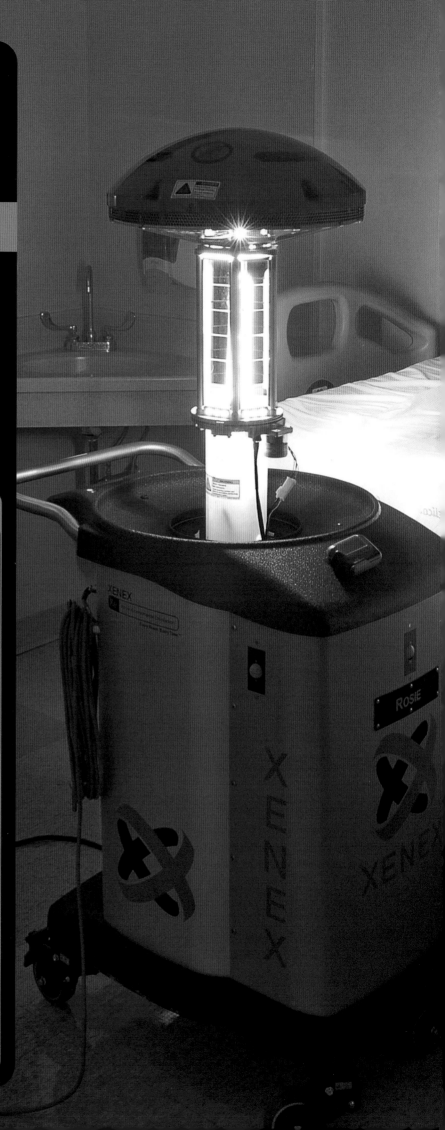

ELECTROMAGNETIC SPECTRUM

UV is one of many types of electromagnetic radiation, all of which can be imagined on a line called the electromagnetic spectrum. On the left side of the spectrum are waves with longer wavelengths (see page 184)—for example, radio waves. Visible light, at the center of the spectrum, is all the wavelengths that we can see with the naked eye. Types of radiation with shorter wavelengths, such as gamma rays, sit on the right side of the spectrum. UV radiation also has shorter wavelengths than visible light, and there are several different types of it.

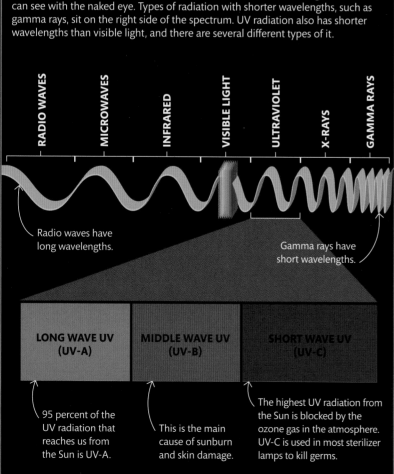

RADIO WAVES   MICROWAVES   INFRARED   VISIBLE LIGHT   ULTRAVIOLET   X-RAYS   GAMMA RAYS

Radio waves have long wavelengths.

Gamma rays have short wavelengths.

LONG WAVE UV (UV-A)	MIDDLE WAVE UV (UV-B)	SHORT WAVE UV (UV-C)

95 percent of the UV radiation that reaches us from the Sun is UV-A.

This is the main cause of sunburn and skin damage.

The highest UV radiation from the Sun is blocked by the ozone gas in the atmosphere. UV-C is used in most sterilizer lamps to kill germs.

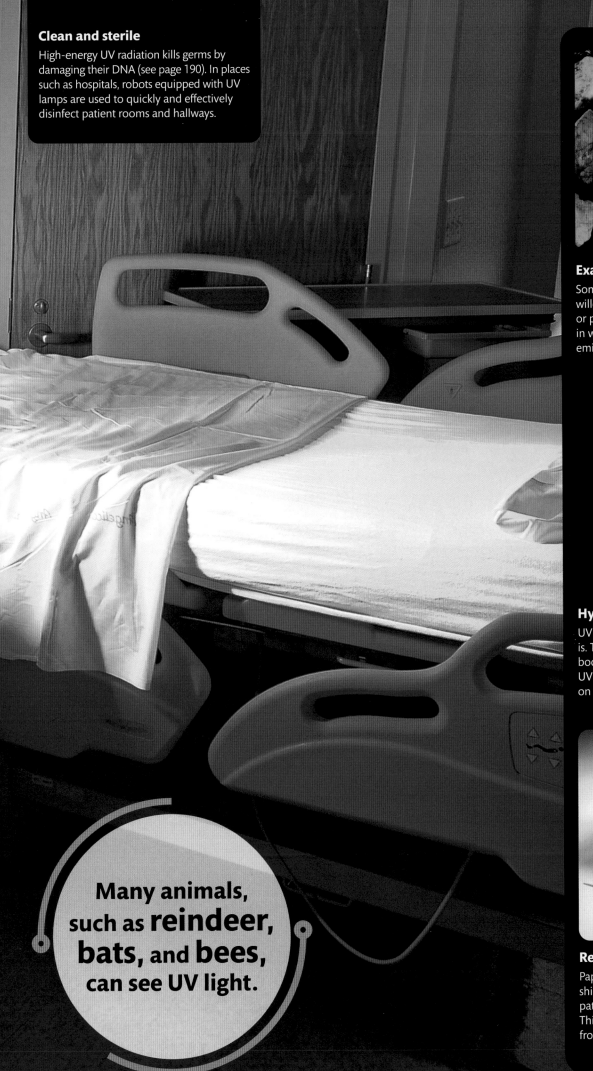

Clean and sterile

High-energy UV radiation kills germs by damaging their DNA (see page 190). In places such as hospitals, robots equipped with UV lamps are used to quickly and effectively disinfect patient rooms and hallways.

Examining rocks

Some minerals glow under UV lamps. The mineral willemite glows green, while fluorite can glow white or purple. This is caused by fluorescence—a process in which a substance absorbs UV radiation and then emits visible light.

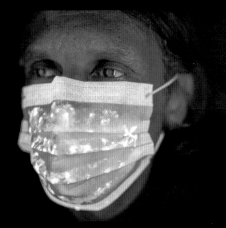

Hygiene checks

UV lamps can be used to check how clean a surface is. The radiation causes things such as bacteria and bodily fluids, including saliva, to become visible. This UV image shows how saliva and other fluids collect on the inside of a face mask.

Real or fake

Paper currency can be checked to see if it is real by shining UV light on it and looking for fluorescing patterns, which have been added by the government. This acts as a security feature that prevents people from making counterfeit money.

Many animals, such as reindeer, bats, and bees, can see UV light.

Diving to the depths

Scuba divers use oxygen tanks underwater to enable them to swim for longer periods. The tanks give them enough time to look for shipwrecks, explore, and study fish up close.

Exhaled carbon dioxide is released into the water.

The oxygen tank is strapped tightly to the diver's back.

Divers breathe through a mouthpiece, which is connected to the tank with an air hose.

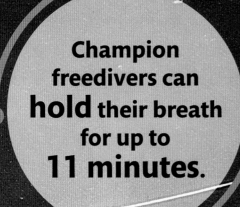

Champion freedivers can hold their breath for up to 11 minutes.

BREATHING UNDERWATER

OXYGEN TANKS

Oxygen is vital for humans to stay alive, so the ability to carry it around is crucial in places where humans can't breathe naturally, such as outer space and underwater. Oxygen gas can be stored in tanks at high pressures and supplied through tubes to the mouth. A device called a regulator helps deliver the oxygen at the right pressure to the user, making it safe to breathe. Oxygen cylinders are also used in hospitals for patients with breathing difficulties.

BREATHING IN SPACE
An astronaut carries an oxygen tank in a backpack, which connects to the helmet. The air on Earth is only 21 percent oxygen, with most of the rest being nitrogen gas. An astronaut's spacesuit is filled with almost 100 percent oxygen.

THE LUNGS

Humans get oxygen by breathing in (inhaling) and channelling air down to their lungs. There, oxygen is transferred into the blood, which then circulates it to the rest of the body. A waste gas, carbon dioxide, passes back into the lungs from the blood and is removed when we breathe out (exhale).

⬇ **AIR FLOWS IN**   ⬆ **AIR FLOWS OUT**

Oxygen is drawn in through the nose and the mouth.

Carbon dioxide is forced out.

Air moves through the windpipe.

The windpipe splits into smaller branches.

At the ends of the branches, gases pass between the lungs and the blood.

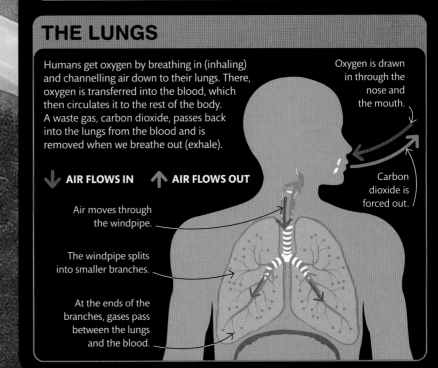

The ropes pass through the skimmers on the ship, which squeeze out the oil to be collected in tanks.

The *Exxon Valdez* oil spill affected 1,300 miles (2,100 km) of coastline and took around **3 years** to clean up.

The ropes are made of materials that attract the oil floating on the water's surface.

Oil floats on top of water, because they don't mix well.

Clean-up operation

In 1989, the *Exxon Valdez* oil tanker struck a reef off Alaska, spilling more than 11 million gallons (41 million liters) of oil in the Pacific Ocean. Skimmers were used to help with the cleanup, removing the layer of oil that floated on the surface of the water. Each had a rope that was dragged across the water's surface to collect oil and pull it back to the boat to be squeezed out. Despite rigorous skimming, some oil still lingered in the water, harming wildlife and causing pollution for decades.

CLEANING UP OIL SPILLS

OIL SKIMMERS

Oil spills from tankers and oil rigs must be removed from the ocean and seas quickly, because they are likely to spread the longer they stay. It is vital to clean up oil spills to minimize their damage to wildlife and the environment. Oil is also a fire hazard and can poison drinking water. Spills are tackled using devices called oil skimmers that remove the oil floating on the water's surface. Oil sticks to the material in the skimmers and is easily removed. Some skimmers only clear away the oil, while others collect it for future use.

ENVIRONMENTAL COST

Spilled oil can stick to the coats of marine creatures and seabirds, making it difficult for them to swim, fly, or breed. It also poisons their food sources, which leads to toxins building up in the food chain, causing long-term problems.

DENSITY

Skimmers work because oil is less dense than water and forms a separate layer on the surface. The density of a substance is how much matter is packed into the space it takes up. The particles in water are more closely packed than those in oil, so water is more dense than oil. Liquids of different densities often form separate layers when mixed together. As a result, oil floats on the surface of water.

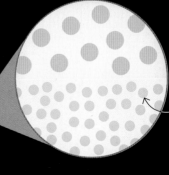

Oil and water do not mix well.

Water molecules are more tightly packed than oil molecules.

STUDYING HABITATS

BIOME DOMES

Earth's surface has many different habitats— from dry deserts to lush forests. Regions with a specific environment where a specialized range of plants and animals have adapted to live are called biomes. In order to study the organisms in these areas, scientists create artificial biomes. The Eden Project in Cornwall, UK, recreates biomes in enclosed domes. It aims to conserve vulnerable plants and raise awareness of the threats they face.

ECO EXPERIMENT

Biosphere 2 in Arizona was originally the site of an experiment to create a self-contained ecosystem involving seven biomes that could then be recreated in space. Humans, plants, and animals lived together for two years, but a sustainable ecosystem was not achieved.

BIOMES

On land, there are four major regions, shown in this pyramid—ranging from the hottest tropical regions to the colder Arctic regions. Factors such as rainfall, humidity, temperature, and altitude all impact the specific habitats within them.

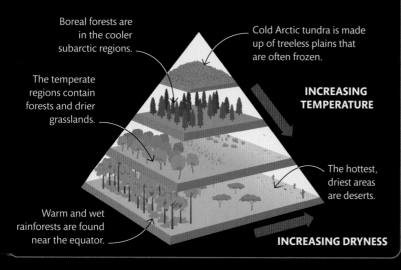

Boreal forests are in the cooler subarctic regions.

Cold Arctic tundra is made up of treeless plains that are often frozen.

The temperate regions contain forests and drier grasslands.

INCREASING TEMPERATURE

The hottest, driest areas are deserts.

Warm and wet rainforests are found near the equator.

INCREASING DRYNESS

Indoor jungle

With more than 1,000 plants, the giant temperature-controlled Rainforest Biome in The Eden Project recreates the conditions of four different environments: Tropical Islands, Southeast Asia, West Africa, and Tropical South America.

At 170,000 sq ft (16,000 sq m) in size, the Rainforest Biome is the world's largest indoor rainforest.

BIOME BUBBLES

The bubble-shaped greenhouses at the Eden Project sit in a giant clay pit. They are made of reinforced steel, covered with an extremely light but strong plastic that allows the light in but traps heat and moisture. Most of the construction was done using sustainably-sourced or recycled materials.

CORAL BLEACHING
Reef-building corals are marine animals that form colonies around rocklike skeletons. Many get their color from microscopic algae living on them. When the ocean warms up, these algae may die and the corals bleach (turn white) and eventually die. Today, the large scale of bleaching due to global warming is a big threat to coral reefs.

Nearly 500 biorock structures have been built around the world.

RESTORING REEFS

BIOROCKS

One of the most diverse ecosystems in the world coral reefs are home to about one-quarter of the fishes in the ocean. However, in recent decades, water pollution, disease, and climate change have weakened and killed corals, threatening these important habitats. This has inspired scientists to develop biorocks—a reef restoration method invented in Jamaica in the 1980s that uses a process called electrolysis to encourage new corals to grow.

ELECTROLYSIS

Biorocks work using a process called electrolysis, in which electricity separates substances from a solution. Two metal pieces called electrodes are placed into the solution, and a source of electricity is connected to them. When this is turned on, negatively charged atoms or molecules (called ions) collect at the positive electrode (called the anode). Positively charged ions collect at the negative electrode (cathode).

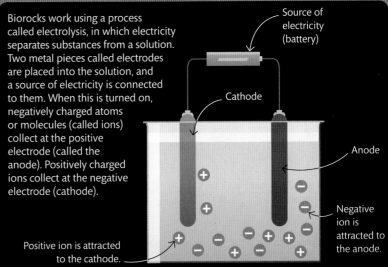

Source of electricity (battery)

Cathode

Anode

Negative ion is attracted to the anode.

Positive ion is attracted to the cathode.

How biorocks work

In a biorock reef, fragments of living coral are attached to a metal cage. When the cage is connected to a source of electricity, it becomes a cathode, and electrolysis begins. The electrolysis causes chemical reactions in the water next to the cage. These allow calcium ions and carbonate ions from the seawater to join together, forming the mineral calcium carbonate on the cage. Corals then use this mineral to build their skeletons.

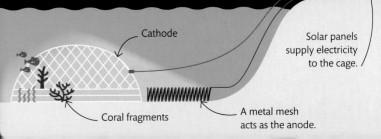

Cathode

Solar panels supply electricity to the cage.

Coral fragments

A metal mesh acts as the anode.

Artificial reef

This cagelike structure in the Indian Ocean, near Indonesia, is covered with calcium carbonate, which encourages threatened corals, such as elkhorn and staghorn, to grow, making the once-dense coral forests come alive again.

Conserving kelp forests

A California bat ray swims through a giant kelp forest in the Channel Islands National Marine Sanctuary. Like coral reefs except they are plants, not animals, kelp forests are an important ocean habitat that researchers around the world are working to conserve.

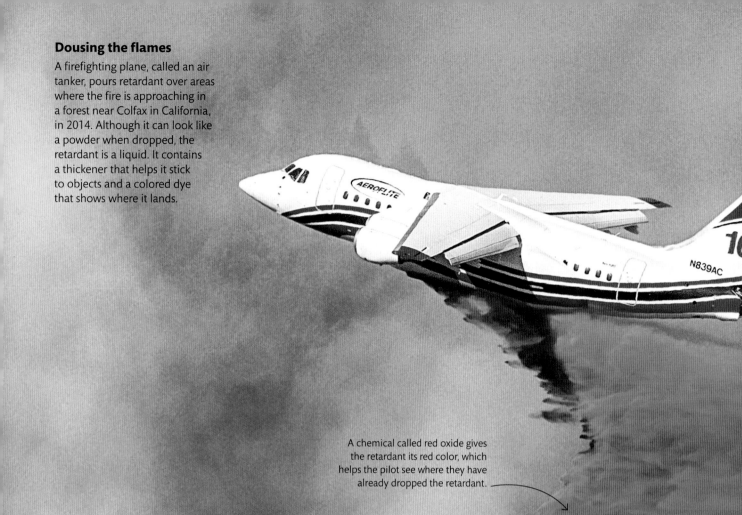

Dousing the flames

A firefighting plane, called an air tanker, pours retardant over areas where the fire is approaching in a forest near Colfax in California, in 2014. Although it can look like a powder when dropped, the retardant is a liquid. It contains a thickener that helps it stick to objects and a colored dye that shows where it lands.

A chemical called red oxide gives the retardant its red color, which helps the pilot see where they have already dropped the retardant.

FIRE EXTINGUISHERS

A small-scale fire can be stopped using a fire extinguisher. This acts like a spray can and quickly expels its contents directly onto a fire. Some contain water, to remove heat, while others can contain carbon dioxide or other fire retardants. Different types of extinguisher are used for different types of fire.

FIGHTING FOREST FIRES

FIRE RETARDANTS

Although forest fires can be a natural part of a forest's life, most forest fires today are caused by humans and can be dangerous for wildlife and people. To slow their spread, fire retardants are sprayed from great heights onto forests. Through a chemical reaction, these retardants coat trees and other plants with a nonflammable substance called char. This removes access to the fuel—one of three things a fire needs to burn

> The largest airtanker can carry up to **24,000** gallons (91,000 liters) of retardant, enough to fill **300** bathtubs.

FIRE TRIANGLE

A fire needs three elements to burn: fuel, heat, and oxygen—as shown by the sides of this triangle. If any one of these is taken away, the fire will not be able to burn.

Heat can be reduced by adding water.

Fire extinguishers cut off a fire's oxygen by smothering it.

Fire retardants prevent fires from accessing fuel.

OXYGEN

HEAT

FUEL

How fire retardants work

For a forest fire to be tackled successfully, the retardant must be sprayed onto vegetation before it catches fire. The substances in the retardant react with a chemical called cellulose in the plants. When fire reaches the plants, the heat breaks down the products of this chemical reaction, forming a protective coating of char—a form of carbon. This stops the fire from getting to the fuel it needs to burn, preventing it from spreading further.

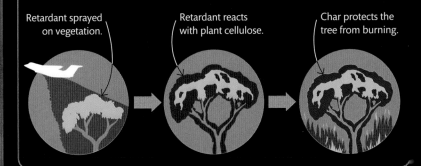

Retardant sprayed on vegetation.

Retardant reacts with plant cellulose.

Char protects the tree from burning.

CAPTURING CARBON
Coal-burning power plants such as Petra Nova in Texas can be fitted with filters to reduce the carbon dioxide they emit. The gas is collected and then compressed and pumped away, often to be stored underground. Scientists are also working to develop machines that can suck carbon dioxide directly from the air.

The Bonn Challenge aims to restore an area of forest the size of 490 million soccer fields by 2030.

Magnificent mangroves
Volunteers plant new mangrove trees in Indonesia. Mangrove forests do not just capture CO₂, but also protect land from flooding and erosion and are an important home for wildlife.

CONTROLLING EMISSIONS

CARBON CAPTURE

Carbon dioxide (CO₂, see page 168) is a greenhouse gas—one of several gases whose presence in the atmosphere keeps our planet's temperature warmer than it would otherwise be. Human activities, such as burning fossil fuels, are increasing the level of CO₂, causing global temperature to rise. Scientists are exploring different ways to reduce CO₂ levels, including planting more trees, which capture carbon dioxide from the air through photosynthesis (see page 52).

GLOBAL HEATING
Measurements show Earth's surface temperatures are rising by about 32°F (0.2°C) every 10 years. This is having many effects on Earth's climate, such as causing Arctic and Antarctic ice to melt. This contributes to rising sea levels.

THE GREENHOUSE EFFECT

Earth is heated by radiation from the Sun, which passes through its atmosphere. Some of it escapes back into space, but some is trapped by gases in the atmosphere in a process similar to how glass in a greenhouse traps heat. This process is called the greenhouse effect. It is important for life on Earth, but if there is too much carbon dioxide in the atmosphere, too much heat is trapped, causing the Earth to heat up.

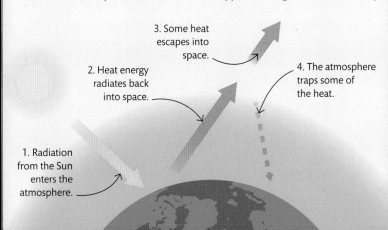

3. Some heat escapes into space.

2. Heat energy radiates back into space.

4. The atmosphere traps some of the heat.

1. Radiation from the Sun enters the atmosphere.

LEARNING AND DISCOVERING

We use science
to understand our world.
Planes are flown into hurricanes
to better predict the weather,
scientists descend into the ocean
and volcanoes to study them, and
telescopes and microscopes let us
see things that are far away or very
small. With scientific tools, we can
track how animals live in the wild
and even see what goes on
inside the human brain.

Tiny divers

Two small submersibles explore a sunken wreck off the coast of the Bahamas while carrying two passengers. This type of submersible can dive as deep as 3,300 ft (1,000 m) and is powered by batteries that last for up to 12 hours.

DEEP DIVING

UNDERWATER VEHICLES

In order to learn more about the ocean's vast unexplored depths, humans have had to construct specialized vehicles to travel in these extreme environments. These are built using strong materials, which make them sturdy enough to bear the immense amounts of pressure created by the water pushing on them. Small crafts, called submersibles, have round edges that allow them to withstand higher pressures, while submarines have streamlined bodies that enable them to move at high speeds and cut through water like a knife. Some can carry people, while others are controlled remotely.

The **deepest** a submersible has dived is **more than 35,000 ft (10,000 m).**

SUBMARINES

Submarines are bigger and more powerful than submersibles and can spend months underwater, carrying enough air and food for large crews. Most submarines are used for military purposes, but they can also be used for exploration, scientific research, and salvaging sunken wrecks.

WATER PRESSURE

Pressure is a measure of how much a force presses on a surface. Air presses on surfaces, and water presses on the surface of submerged objects. Pressure is often measured in units called atmospheres (atm)—1 atm is the pressure exerted by air at sea level. The deeper you dive into the ocean, the greater the pressure, because of the increased weight of the water above you. For every 33 ft (10 m) of depth, the water pressure increases by 1 atm. So vehicles that dive very deep have to be very strong.

Most divers only dive up to a depth of 99 ft (30 m), beyond which the pressure can be harmful to the body.

Some submersibles can dive down to 1,640 ft (500 m).

Some submarines can dive to a depth of 0.6 miles (1 km).

Some submersibles can reach depths of nearly 6 miles (10 km), withstanding a pressure of 1,000 atm.

Into the inferno

An explorer climbs down into an active volcano on an island in Vanuatu. Anyone descending into such an extreme environment must wear a heat-resistant suit and a mask to protect against poisonous gases.

INTO THE VOLCANO

FORECASTING VOLCANIC ERUPTIONS

When volcanoes erupt, they spit out dangerous hot ash, lava, and poisonous gases. In 2019, more than 29 million people were living near active volcanoes, so predicting eruptions is important. While it is difficult to know exactly when a volcano will erupt, vulcanologists gather clues by measuring earthquakes in volcanic regions, using satellites in space to monitor volcanoes and their surroundings, and even climbing down into them to collect gas samples.

Lava from a volcano can reach 2,282°F (1,250°C)— **12 times** hotter than boiling water.

VOLCANIC ACTIVITY

Volcanoes can either be extinct, meaning unlikely to erupt again; active, which means they erupt frequently or dormant, meaning they have not erupted for some time. The Chaitén Volcano in Chile hadn't erupted for more than 350 years before erupting in 2008.

HOW VOLCANOES FORM

A volcano is formed where molten rock breaks through Earth's crust. Below ground, molten rock is called magma, and above ground it is called lava. Erupting magma forms ash and a rock called pumice. Layers of cooled lava, pumice, and ash can form a volcanic mountain.

Clouds of ash and dust form during a volcanic eruption.

Hot lava can flow, or pumice and ash can explode, from the crater.

Lava flows down slope.

The magma chamber below the volcano contains molten rock.

Layers of cooled lava, pumice, and ash.

STUDYING STORMS
WEATHER PLANES

Scientists record and analyze data to forecast the behavior of many weather phenomena, including tropical cyclones (also known as hurricanes). The US National Oceanic and Atmospheric Administration (NOAA) has specially equipped airplanes that fly through these storms to gather data and help scientists understand and predict their activity. Two of NOAA's largest planes, known as Hurricane Hunters, are flying laboratories with radars that can scan the storm and provide real-time information to scientists.

A parachute slows down the dropsonde's descent, allowing it to gather as much data as possible.

DROPSONDES
As the Hurricane Hunters fly through the storm, they deploy small capsules called dropsondes. These are packed with sensors that measure pressure, temperature, humidity, and wind direction, and transmit the information back to the plane.

HURRICANES

Tropical cyclones—also known as hurricanes or typhoons—are large rotating storms of wind, rain, and cloud. They form over tropical oceans where warm, rising air causes an area of low pressure. The air around the center then spirals inward and up, forming bands of rainclouds that are buffeted around in a spiral pattern by ferociously strong winds.

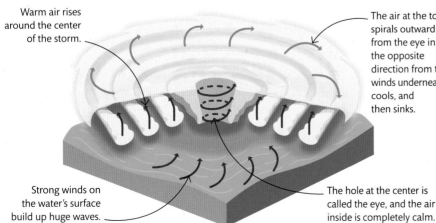

Warm air rises around the center of the storm.

The air at the top spirals outward from the eye in the opposite direction from the winds underneath, cools, and then sinks.

Strong winds on the water's surface build up huge waves.

The hole at the center is called the eye, and the air inside is completely calm.

In the eye of the storm
The two large Hurricane Hunters are propeller-driven Lockheed WP-3D Orion airplanes. They criss-cross through the storm's center several times to gather data about changing wind and pressure conditions. Each mission can last for up to 10 hours.

The tube contains a GPS antenna to send information back to the plane.

A large dome on the plane's underside houses a radar that helps produce accurate pictures of the storm's clouds and rainfall.

Tropical storms rotate clockwise in the southern hemisphere and counterclockwise in the northern hemisphere.

Hurricane Hunters can fly at altitudes of up to 10,000 ft (3,048 m).

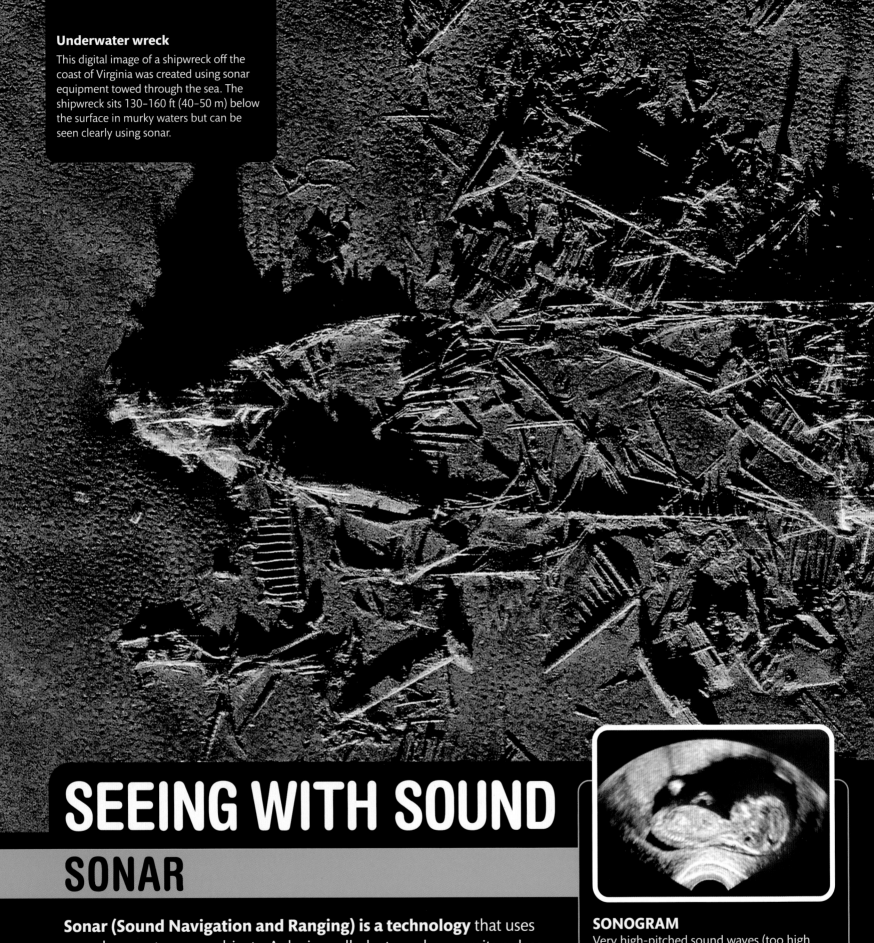

SEEING WITH SOUND

SONAR

Sonar (Sound Navigation and Ranging) is a technology that uses sound waves to sense objects. A device called a transducer emits pulses of sound waves and another called a detector listens for their echoes, which are used to measure the distance to the object. Using this information, a computer can also make a model of the object. Sonar is often used underwater—where sound can travel great distances—for mapping the seafloor and avoiding obstacles.

SONOGRAM
Very high-pitched sound waves (too high for humans to hear) are used in healthcare, in a technique similar to underwater sonar. Sound waves are reflected off different parts in the human body to build an image called a sonogram. These images can be used to check the development of unborn babies.

Bats and dolphins use **echolocation** (their own form of sonar) to navigate through their surroundings.

SOUND WAVES

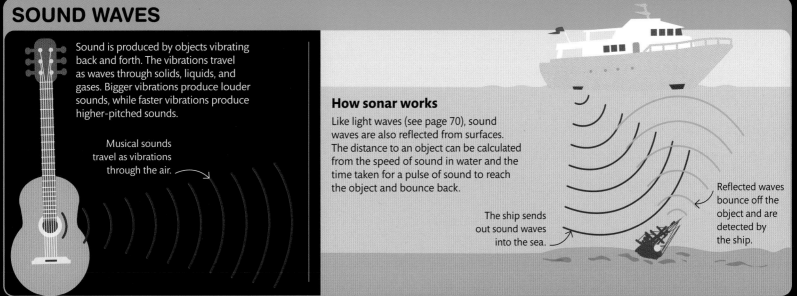

Sound is produced by objects vibrating back and forth. The vibrations travel as waves through solids, liquids, and gases. Bigger vibrations produce louder sounds, while faster vibrations produce higher-pitched sounds.

Musical sounds travel as vibrations through the air.

How sonar works

Like light waves (see page 70), sound waves are also reflected from surfaces. The distance to an object can be calculated from the speed of sound in water and the time taken for a pulse of sound to reach the object and bounce back.

The ship sends out sound waves into the sea.

Reflected waves bounce off the object and are detected by the ship.

CLUES TO THE CLIMATE

ICE CORES

When an ice sheet or a glacier forms over many years, gases from the air are trapped inside as tiny bubbles. These can provide clues about Earth's climate at different points in the past. Experts drill deep into the ice to extract long icy cylinders and examine them to find out which gases were in the atmosphere at different times in the history of our planet. This can tell us how the levels of greenhouse gases—gases that trap heat and make Earth's surface warmer—have varied over time, changing the climate.

1 Drilling into the ice
In the freezing Antarctic, scientists use a special drill to extract a cylindrical block of ice from the ice sheets. The oldest ice can be found in the center of an ice sheet, so the drilling must take place far from the coast and far from any research station.

ATMOSPHERIC GASES

Earth's atmosphere is mostly made up of nitrogen and oxygen, along with small amounts of other trace gases, including helium, ozone, and carbon dioxide (a greenhouse gas). But the proportion of these gases has changed throughout history. Scientists can count layers in the ice like rings in a tree to determine how old each layer of ice is. Through this, they have discovered that since the Industrial Revolution in the 1760s, the levels of carbon dioxide in the atmosphere have been rising steadily.

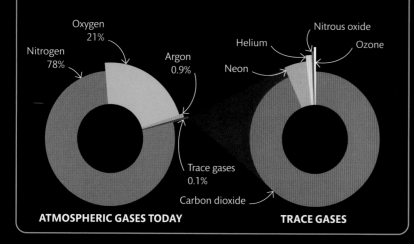

Oxygen 21%

Nitrogen 78%

Argon 0.9%

Nitrous oxide

Helium

Ozone

Neon

Trace gases 0.1%

Carbon dioxide

ATMOSPHERIC GASES TODAY

TRACE GASES

The oldest ice core, found in Antarctica, is nearly **2 million** years old.

2 Preparing the core for study

The block of ice is carefully removed from the drill and prepared as a sample. Ice cores must be kept below −0.4°F (−18°C) to prevent the gases in the air bubbles from escaping the ice. The cores are transported in a mobile freezer.

3 Storage

The cores, which can be miles long, are cut into small 3.3-ft (1-m) sections and stored at −32.8°F (−36°C). This lab in Colorado stores 11.8 miles (19 km) of ice cores for research.

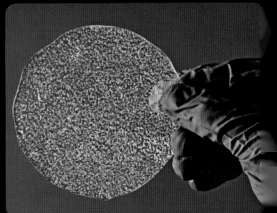

4 Analyzing samples

Researchers cut thin slices from the cores to analyze the trapped air bubbles in detail. Each slice provides a snapshot of the atmosphere and climate conditions at a particular point in history, including information about volcanic activity and wind patterns.

STUDYING THE ATMOSPHERE

WEATHER BALLOONS

Earth is surrounded by a layer of gases called the atmosphere. The two main gases are nitrogen and oxygen, with small amounts of others. The atmosphere supports life on Earth by absorbing harmful radiation from the Sun, trapping heat, and generating pressure, which allows liquid water to exist on Earth. Understanding the atmosphere can tell us about weather patterns, pollution, climate change, and more. One way to study it is using weather balloons, which can carry scientific instruments high up into the atmosphere and send back data to scientists on Earth.

Gathering data

Weather balloons carry scientific instruments that can measure atmospheric pressure, humidity, and temperature. They can also identify the gases present at different heights in the atmosphere. This time-lapse photo shows a balloon being released by scientists in Antarctica. It is carrying an instrument to monitor ozone levels.

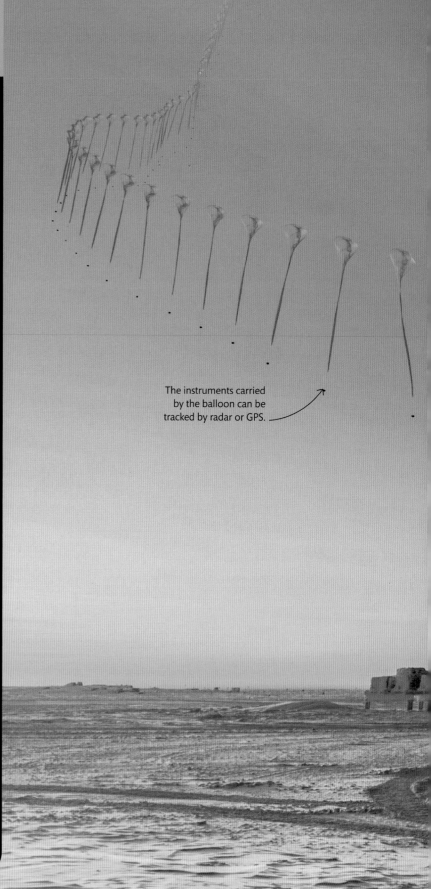

The instruments carried by the balloon can be tracked by radar or GPS.

EARTH'S ATMOSPHERE

The atmosphere is made up of distinct layers that become less dense as the distance from Earth's surface increases, until the outer layer merges with space. The closest layer to Earth is the troposphere, which contains the air we breathe.

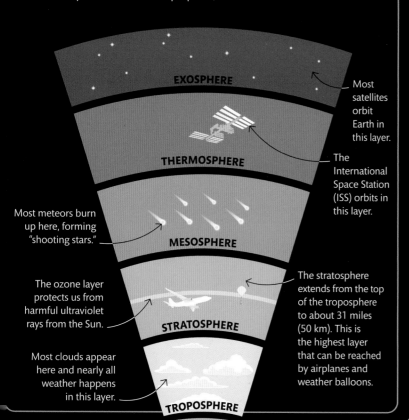

EXOSPHERE

Most satellites orbit Earth in this layer.

THERMOSPHERE

The International Space Station (ISS) orbits in this layer.

Most meteors burn up here, forming "shooting stars."

MESOSPHERE

The ozone layer protects us from harmful ultraviolet rays from the Sun.

The stratosphere extends from the top of the troposphere to about 31 miles (50 km). This is the highest layer that can be reached by airplanes and weather balloons.

STRATOSPHERE

Most clouds appear here and nearly all weather happens in this layer.

TROPOSPHERE

Some weather balloons can reach **heights** of more than **32 miles** (52 km).

TRACKING STORMS
Weather balloons can measure wind speeds and collect information about other atmospheric conditions. This data can provide early warnings of severe weather conditions, such as this tornado in Oklahoma.

The balloon is usually filled with helium or hydrogen, both of which are lighter than air.

SCANNING THE SKIES

TELESCOPES

For centuries, humans have looked at the skies and studied objects in space. But the invention and development of the telescope has enabled us to look farther into the Universe, making distant objects ever more visible. In a telescope, light from a distant object such as a comet, planet, or star is gathered and brought into focus, forming a bright image, which can then be magnified. There are different types of telescopes—reflecting telescopes use curved mirrors and refracting telescopes use lenses. Some telescopes detect other types of electromagnetic radiation, such as radio waves.

Eye on space

Perched on top of an extinct volcano in Spain's Canary Islands, the Gran Telescopio Canarias—the world's largest reflecting telescope—is located far away from pollution and city lights, making it ideal for observing objects in space in great detail. Its primary mirror is made up of 36 hexagonal segments, which collectively behave like a single giant mirror 34 ft (10.4 m) in diameter.

TELESCOPE MIRRORS

Light rays, or waves, reflect, or bounce off, objects (see page 70). Mirrors reflect nearly all the light that hits them, and curved mirrors can be used to focus light to a point. A concave mirror is curved inward like a bowl, while a convex mirror is curved outward like a dome.

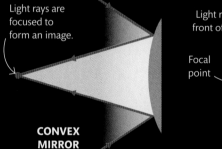

Light rays are focused to form an image.

Light rays focus in front of the mirror.

Focal point

CONVEX MIRROR

CONCAVE MIRROR

How reflecting telescopes work

A reflecting telescope contains a large, concave primary mirror and a smaller secondary mirror. The primary mirror receives the incoming light from an object in space and focuses it on the secondary mirror. The secondary mirror then reflects this light toward a camera, allowing the telescope to take pictures of the distant object.

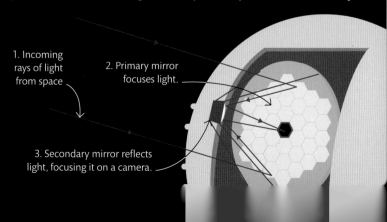

1. Incoming rays of light from space

2. Primary mirror focuses light.

3. Secondary mirror reflects light, focusing it on a camera.

The Gran Telescopio Canarias can collect light that has traveled across space for **millions** of years.

SPACE SIGNALS

Radio telescopes detect radio waves emitted by objects such as galaxies and stars. The world's largest single-dish radio telescope is located in Guizhou, China. Its large bowl-shaped dish is made up of 4,450 panels that move together to focus the dish on an object in space.

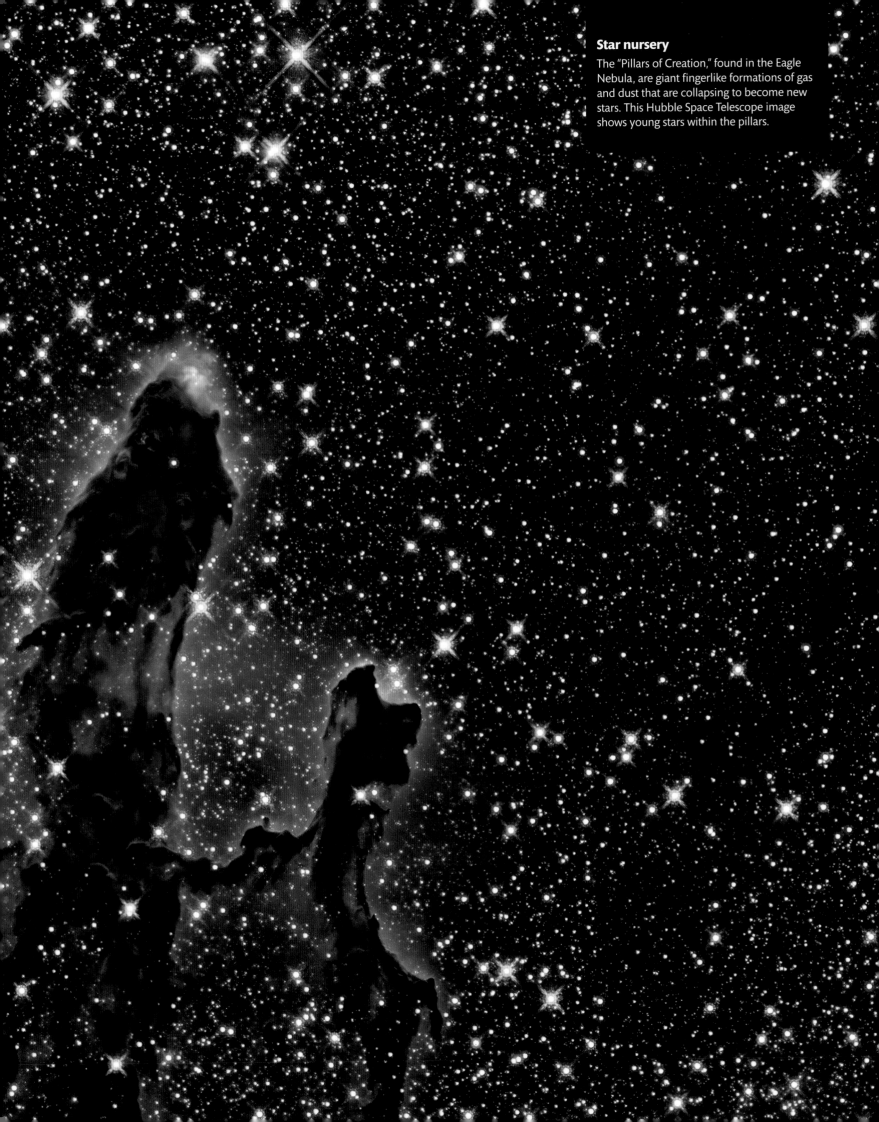

Star nursery
The "Pillars of Creation," found in the Eagle Nebula, are giant fingerlike formations of gas and dust that are collapsing to become new stars. This Hubble Space Telescope image shows young stars within the pillars.

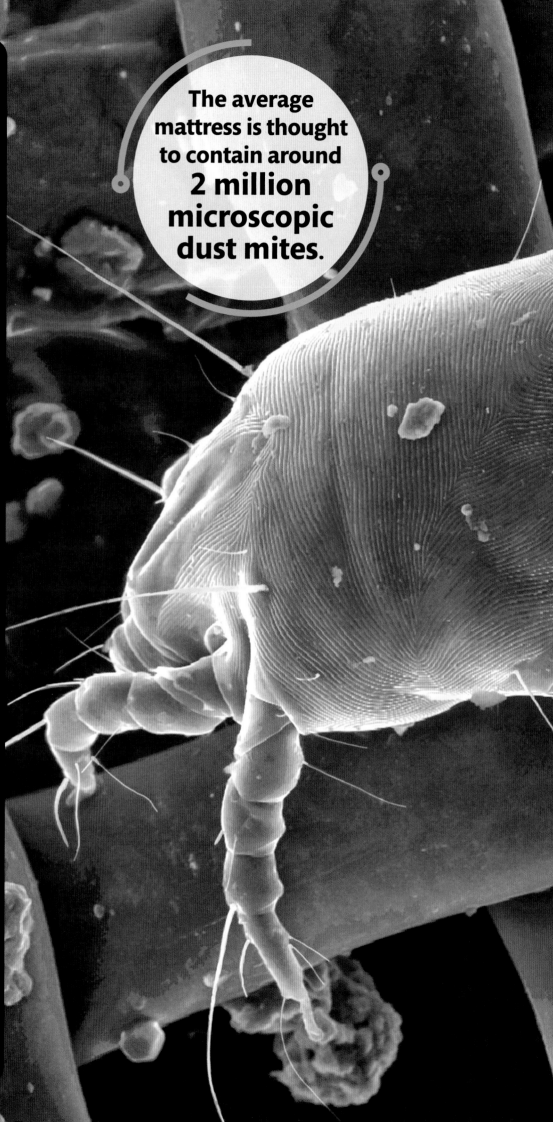

1 On the surface
To the unaided eye, this carpet looks perfectly normal and clean, but zooming in with a microscope reveals the hidden world of dirt, dust, and mysterious creatures crawling beneath our feet.

2 A little closer
Under a microscope, the individual fibers of the carpet can be seen clearly, as well as tiny bits of dust and some microscopic animals. This level of magnification is possible with a light microscope.

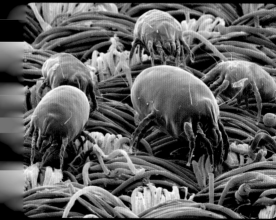

3 Seeing the invisible
Under a more advanced microscope, tiny dust mites, which are distant relatives of spiders, become visible. These creatures feast on tiny flakes of dead skin that humans constantly shed and are a common cause of allergies.

The average mattress is thought to contain around **2 million microscopic dust mites.**

ZOOMING IN

MICROSCOPES

Microscopes have been used by humans for hundreds of years to study the smallest parts of our world—from the cells in our own bodies to tiny microorganisms smaller than a grain of sand. Different microscopes can show different levels of detail. Light microscopes use lenses and can magnify things 1,500 times, while more powerful electron microscopes use beams of tiny particles called electrons, which can help magnify objects up to a million times their original size.

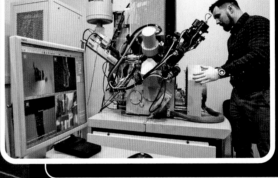

SEM

At a research laboratory in Russia, this scientist is using a type of microscope called a scanning electron microscope (SEM) to analyze fragments of an object. SEMs can be used to study bacteria, to tell apart rock samples, and even to help assemble tiny parts of computers.

ELECTRONS

Atoms are the building blocks of the Universe—tiny structures making up everything around us. They are made of three smaller particles. An atom has a central hub, or nucleus, containing particles called protons (which have a positive charge) and neutrons (neutral particles with no charge). Tiny negatively charged particles called electrons zip along in orbits around the nucleus. Different atoms contain different numbers of these particles. Electrons are used in a scanning electron microscope.

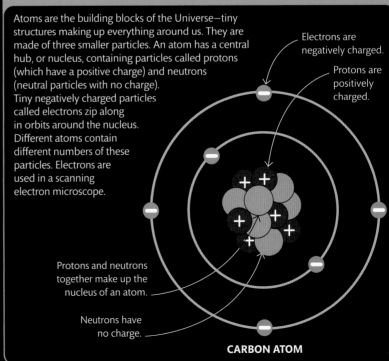

Electrons are negatively charged.

Protons are positively charged.

Protons and neutrons together make up the nucleus of an atom.

Neutrons have no charge.

CARBON ATOM

4 Close-up creatures
Under the high magnification of an electron microscope, the details of a dust mite—only about a quarter of a millimeter long—can be seen. Scientists can learn about the creature's anatomy from this close-up view.

UNLOCKING THE PAST

DATING FOSSILS

All matter is made up of atoms (see page 177). For each element, there are several different forms, called isotopes, each with a different number of neutrons. Some isotopes are radioactive, which means they break apart, or decay. When animals or plants die, they leave behind many isotopes in their bodies, including carbon isotopes. By measuring the levels of these isotopes in a fossil, scientists can discover when the organism died.

THE CARBON CYCLE

The element carbon, most often in the form of CO_2, constantly passes between living things and the air, soil, and water whenever living things breathe, eat, or die. This is the carbon cycle. When something dies, it stops taking in carbon, so the mix of carbon isotopes is fixed. As time passes, some of the isotopes decay, so measuring their concentration allows scientists to date when the animal or plant died.

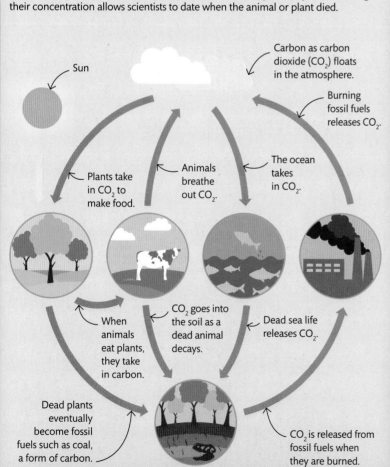

Sun

Carbon as carbon dioxide (CO_2) floats in the atmosphere.

Burning fossil fuels releases CO_2.

Plants take in CO_2 to make food.

Animals breathe out CO_2.

The ocean takes in CO_2.

When animals eat plants, they take in carbon.

CO_2 goes into the soil as a dead animal decays.

Dead sea life releases CO_2.

Dead plants eventually become fossil fuels such as coal, a form of carbon.

CO_2 is released from fossil fuels when they are burned.

Dinosaur fossils

These fossils found in Sahatsakhan, Thailand, belong to a type of plant-eating dinosaur called a sauropod. Back in the lab, scientists will study the uranium isotopes in the fossils to calculate how many millions of years ago the dinosaur died. Dinosaur remains are too old for carbon dating, as the carbon isotopes will have fully decayed.

The oldest fossils dated are from microbes that lived **3.5 billion** years ago.

EXAMINING ARTIFACTS
CT SCANS

A CT (computed tomography) scanner can use X-rays to reveal the insides of an object, usually the organs of a human body. The machine sends X-rays through the object at different angles. Measurements of how much X-ray passes through are combined to produce a 3D picture. Doctors can use these machines to examine their patients, while archaeologists can see inside ancient artifacts such as mummies and sarcophagi without taking them apart.

MAKING A MODEL

X-ray images are taken from all around the object and then processed by a computer to generate detailed cross-sectional images, called slices, and 3D models of structures within the object. Seen here is the computer-generated model of the head of an Ancient Egyptian mummy.

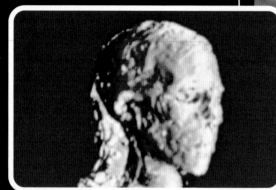

X-RAYS

X-rays are a type of invisible radiation (see page 142) that can pass through most materials. As X-rays travel through an object like a human body, different amounts of radiation are absorbed by different tissues of the body. Dense material such as bone absorbs more than soft material such as muscle. A detector measures the strength of X-rays that make it through the body in each direction, and a computer uses these measurements to create a 3D image.

In a CT scanner, the X-ray source rotates to capture images from all angles.

X-RAY BEAM

The X-ray beam passes through the patient.

The X-ray detector, which picks up the radiation, rotates along with the source.

Uncovering secrets

The 3,000-year-old mummy of Nesperennub, an Egyptian priest, is seen here being moved into a CT scanner. A study of the completed scans revealed a tiny pit on the inside of his skull, which suggests he might have died due to a major illness that affected his bones.

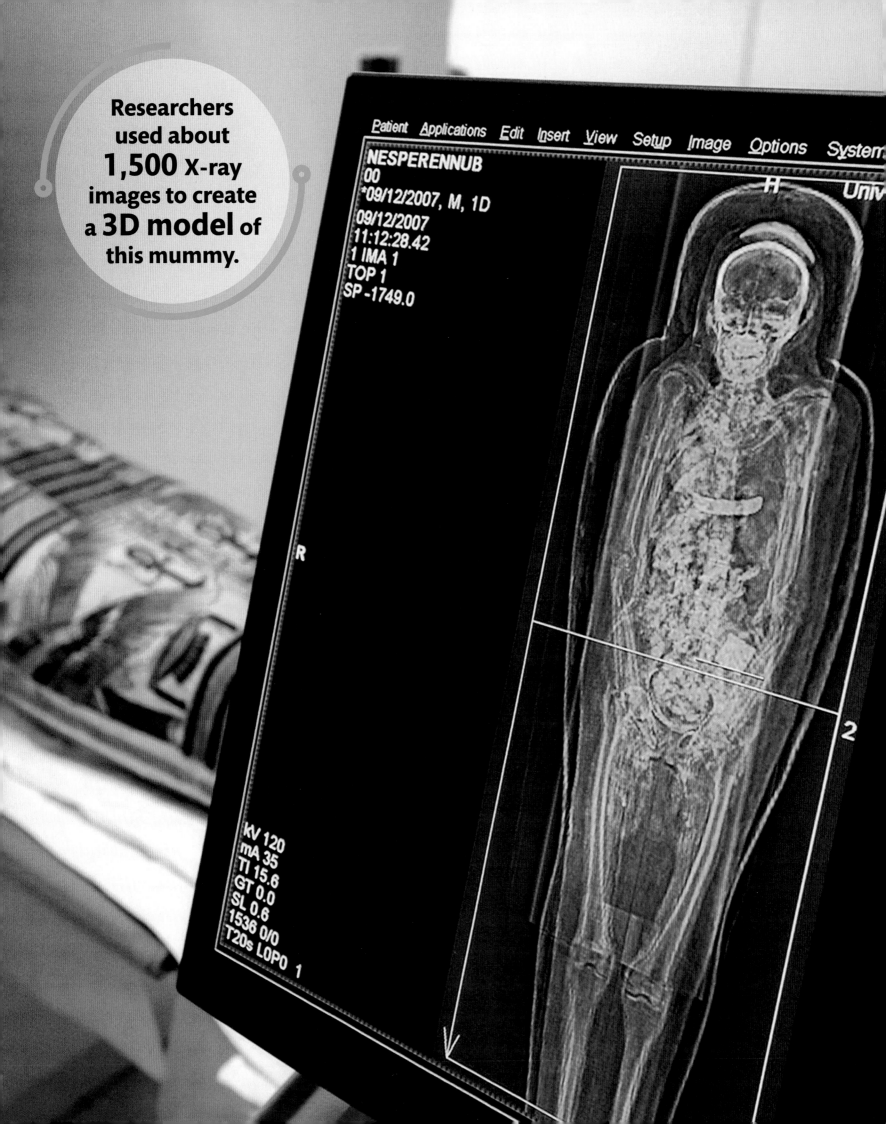

Researchers used about **1,500** X-ray images to create a **3D model** of this mummy.

MEETING OUR ANCESTORS

REBUILDING FOSSILS

Studying the fossil remains of early humans and their relatives can allow us to find out more about our ancestors and how they lived. By using new techniques, such as scanning, 3D printing, and DNA analysis, scientists can recreate what our ancient relatives might have looked like by making detailed models. These then help them understand how different human species evolved over millions of years.

ART AND SCIENCE

Bringing fossils to life is called paleoart, as it combines the science of paleobiology with art. Here, French paleoartist Élisabeth Daynès works on a reconstruction of extinct human relative *Australopithecus africanus*.

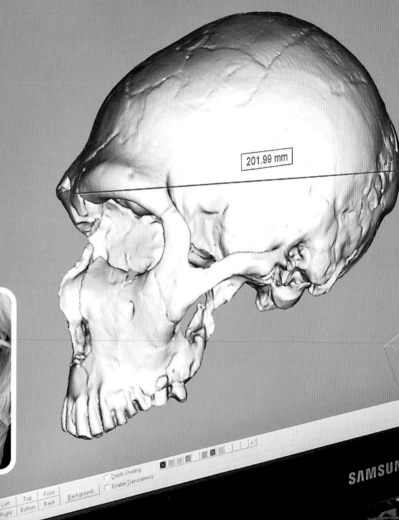

1 **Scanning the bones**
Using a scanner, scientists can take measurements from this delicate fossil of a Neanderthal skull and create a virtual fossil on a computer. The structure can then be 3D printed, ready to be worked on.

201.99 mm

SAMSUNG

HUMAN EVOLUTION

Evolution is the process of how living things change over long periods of time. When lots of small changes make a type of organism very different, it becomes a new species. The first human species evolved from ancient apes 3.3 millions of years ago (MYA). Our species, *Homo sapiens*, did not evolve until around 300,000 years ago, but it is the only one to survive to the present day. The diagram below shows a few of our relatives and the times during which they lived.

Australopithecus africanus 3.3. MYA

Homo habilis 2.4–1.6 MYA

Homo erectus 1.8 MYA– 180,000 BCE

Homo neanderthalensis 400,000– 40,000 BCE

Homo sapiens 300,000 BCE– present

More than 6,000 fossils of early humans have been discovered so far.

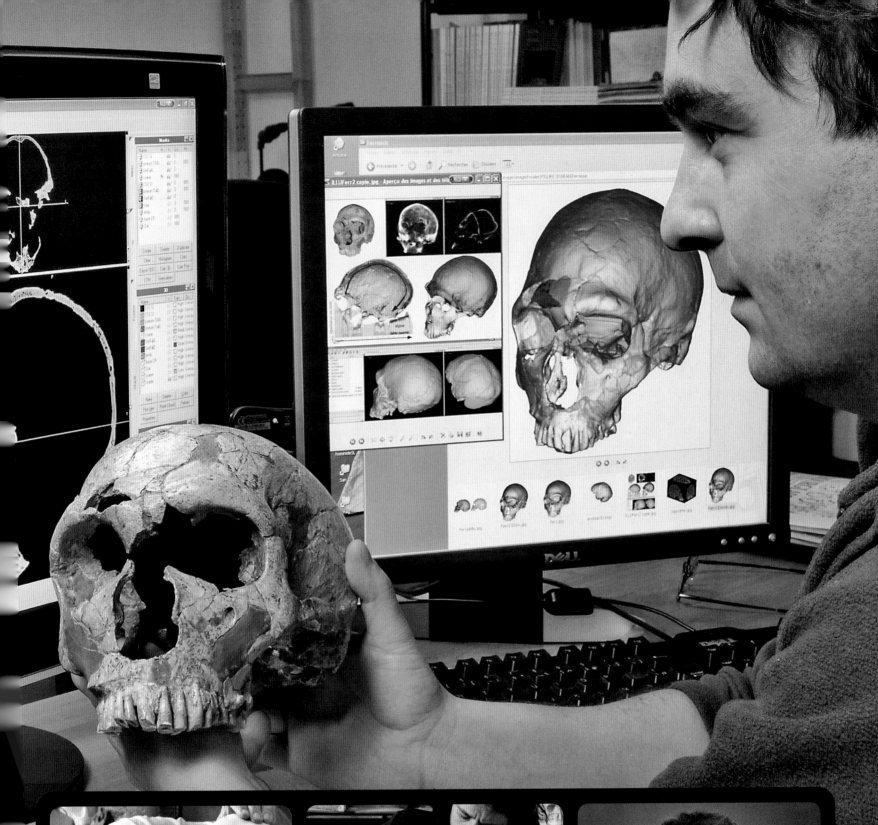

2 Adding muscles

Following general rules about the thickness of muscle and skin in different parts of the human skull—as well as a bit of guesswork— the structure of the face is built up.

3 Making a cast

When the face is finished, complete with muscles; skin; and even incredibly specific details such as scratches, veins, and facial expressions, a cast (mold) is made. This is then used to make

4 Final touches

Finally, hair and colors are added, bringing the model to life. The skin's coloring can be worked out using knowledge of the species' environment. Analysis of DNA evidence

MEASURING HEAT

THERMAL IMAGING

All objects emit heat in the form of infrared radiation. This is invisible to the human eye, but thermal imaging cameras equipped with special sensors can detect it. These map the differences in temperatures and turn the readings into visible color images. Cool objects appear blue or purple, while warmer objects look red or yellow. These cameras are useful for monitoring people and detecting other objects when visibility is poor.

Some **snakes** can detect infrared radiation, allowing them to **hunt** in the **dark**.

NIGHT VISION GOGGLES

Unlike thermal cameras, night vision goggles do not work in absolute darkness. They intensify any faint visible light and then translate it into a clearer green-tinted final image.

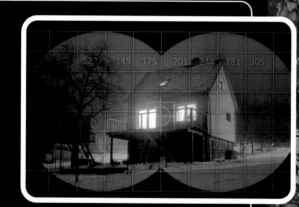

MEASURING WAVES

Infrared is a form of electromagnetic radiation (see page 142), which, like the visible light we see, travels as waves. All waves are different, and we can measure them by looking at their wavelength (the distance between two peaks), their amplitude (the wave's height), and their frequency (the number of waves per second). Infrared waves cannot be seen by the naked eye, because they have a longer wavelength than visible light.

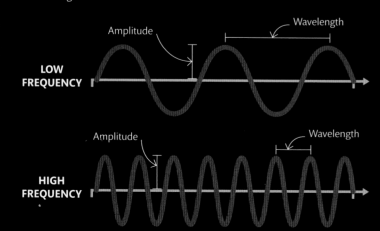

Amplitude

Wavelength

LOW FREQUENCY

Amplitude

Wavelength

HIGH FREQUENCY

COLD   HOT

Firefighting

Thermal cameras are used by firefighters to see through smoke or darkness, allowing them to quickly locate trapped people in critical situations. They can also be used to identify where the fire first started.

Electrical maintenance

Problems in electrical systems often result in abnormal heating of equipment. Thermal cameras are used to check for overheating and identify problems before they become dangerous.

Airport scanning

Thermal imaging is used at busy transportation hubs, such as airports, for security and to monitor public health. It can reveal passengers traveling with fevers, helping prevent the spread of infectious diseases.

Studying wildlife

Humans have limited night vision, but thermal imaging cameras let us see even in complete darkness. By making tiny temperature differences visible, they reveal this owl in detail.

MOVING MACHINES
ROBOT CAMERAS

Robots are machines programmed to carry out a series of actions on their own. They are often used for tasks that are repetitive, dangerous, or impossible for humans to do themselves, such as capturing useful footage of animals without disturbing them. Robots that mimic animals and plants are known as biomimetic robots. They are an ideal way to monitor wildlife, and allow scientists to learn more about animal behavior and social habits.

ROBOTS FOR THERAPY
Robots are increasingly playing an important role in health and social care. Seen here is Paro, a therapeutic robot resembling a baby harp seal. Its sensors detect touch and voices, and it wriggles and makes sounds in response. It has been proven to lift moods and reduce distress in patients and nursing home residents.

This robot entered a troop of more than **120 langur monkeys** and was accepted as one of their own.

ROBOTICS

A robot is a moving machine that can sense things such as movement or sound in its environment and carry out actions in response. It receives information through input devices called sensors, such as light detectors. The information is processed in a central processing unit (CPU), which is the robot's brain. The CPU sends instructions to output devices, such as speakers.

INPUT ➡ **CPU** ➡ **OUTPUT**

1. A sensor detects sound and movement in its surroundings and sends this information to the CPU.

2. The CPU processes the data and sends instructions to the output device to respond.

3. The output device activates motors and cameras as directed by the CPU.

Robot monkey

The spy camera in the robot monkey has infrared sensors for detecting nearby motion (input). In response to this input, motors in the robot's neck are activated, helping the animal turn its head. This design allows the robot to film activity in its surroundings.

Made of synthetic materials, the robot's fur resembles langur hair.

Ultra-high-definition (UHD) spy cameras are embedded in the robot's eyes.

Movement is triggered by infrared sensors if another animal comes close.

Pepper Parlor

A line of humanlike robots called Pepper take food and drink orders at the Pepper Parlor café in Tokyo, Japan. The robots also interact with customers at their tables, offering a range of games and activities.

IDENTIFYING CRIMINALS

DNA ANALYSIS

Forensics is the use of science to work out what happened at the scene of a crime. Forensic scientists study many different types of evidence, such as traces of blood, fingerprints, footprints, and other marks. They are also able to analyze DNA—the set of genetic instructions we all contain. Every person's DNA is unique (apart from that of identical twins). It is found in almost every cell of our body, so we easily lose bits by shedding flakes of skin and hairs or by losing blood.

GENETIC TESTING

DNA testing is not just useful for the police. Home DNA testing kits use a person's spit to extract their DNA, allowing people to find out who they are related to and their wider ancestry. Doctors also use genetic tests to look for the causes of diseases.

DNA

DNA—short for deoxyribonucleic acid—is like a biological bar code, a unique recipe for making each one of us who we are. It is found inside cells of the body, in the nucleus—a cell's control center—and has a ladder-shaped structure called a double helix. The "rungs" of the ladder are made up of four different chemicals called bases, shown here in different colors.

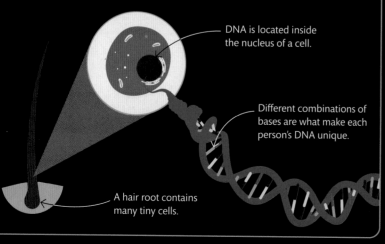

DNA is located inside the nucleus of a cell.

Different combinations of bases are what make each person's DNA unique.

A hair root contains many tiny cells.

CRIME SCE

EVIDEN

1 The scene of the crime

Forensic specialists comb crime scenes for samples of DNA by looking for traces of blood, saliva, and hair, and by collecting clothes and other items. Everything a person has touched could have their DNA on it.

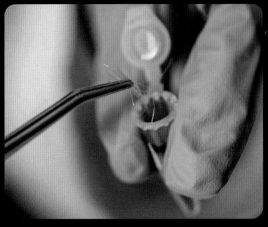

2 Collecting samples

Anything that could contain DNA, such as hair, is carefully collected and sent to specialists. Swabs are also taken from any suspects, from which their DNA can be extracted for comparison.

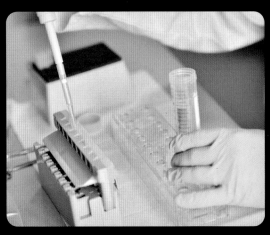

3 In the lab

Once the samples arrive in the lab, scientists extract the DNA from cells in the root of the hairs and multiply it so there is enough to analyze. This DNA is run through machines that can read the unique genetic code it contains.

The DNA inside a human cell would be **6.5 ft (2 m) long** if fully stretched out.

4 Analyzing the DNA

A person's DNA acts like a fingerprint, and scientists can make a printout of its unique code. The DNA from the crime scene can then be compared to the DNA of suspects to look for any matches.

BRAIN SURVEY

MRI SCANS

The human body is an incredible and complex structure that scientists still seek to properly understand. But it is difficult to study how the living body works without surgery. However, magnetic resonance imaging (MRI) can offer a unique view inside. It produces more detailed scans than X-rays, showing not only bones, but soft tissues as well. MRI machines work by using powerful magnets and radio signals. A computer turns the radio signals into images to create a detailed picture of our insides— even the brain beneath the thick skull.

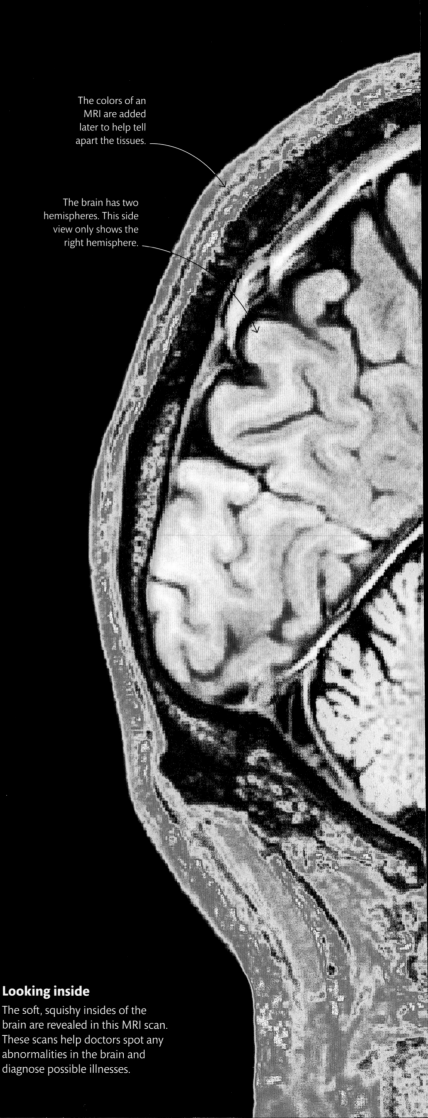

The colors of an MRI are added later to help tell apart the tissues.

The brain has two hemispheres. This side view only shows the right hemisphere.

BRAIN ACTIVITY

In 2015, neuroscientist Rebecca Saxe took this MRI scan of herself and her baby to compare adult and infant brains. She later added the results of another scan to the image, which show the spots in the brain that light up when recognizing faces.

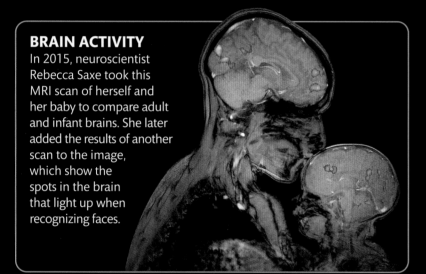

THE HUMAN BRAIN

The brain is a network of billions of cells called neurons that communicate with each other. It is the center of the nervous system, processing information from the senses and controlling muscles. The biggest part, called the cerebrum, is divided into areas called lobes, each specializing in particular functions.

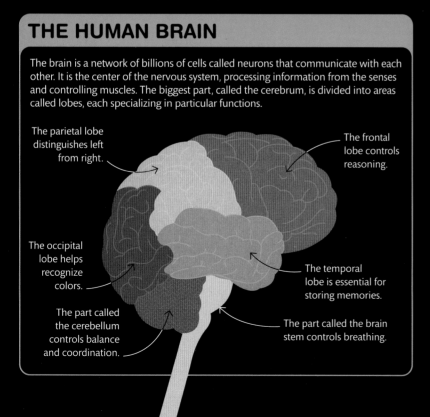

The parietal lobe distinguishes left from right.

The frontal lobe controls reasoning.

The occipital lobe helps recognize colors.

The temporal lobe is essential for storing memories.

The part called the cerebellum controls balance and coordination.

The part called the brain stem controls breathing.

Looking inside

The soft, squishy insides of the brain are revealed in this MRI scan. These scans help doctors spot any abnormalities in the brain and diagnose possible illnesses.

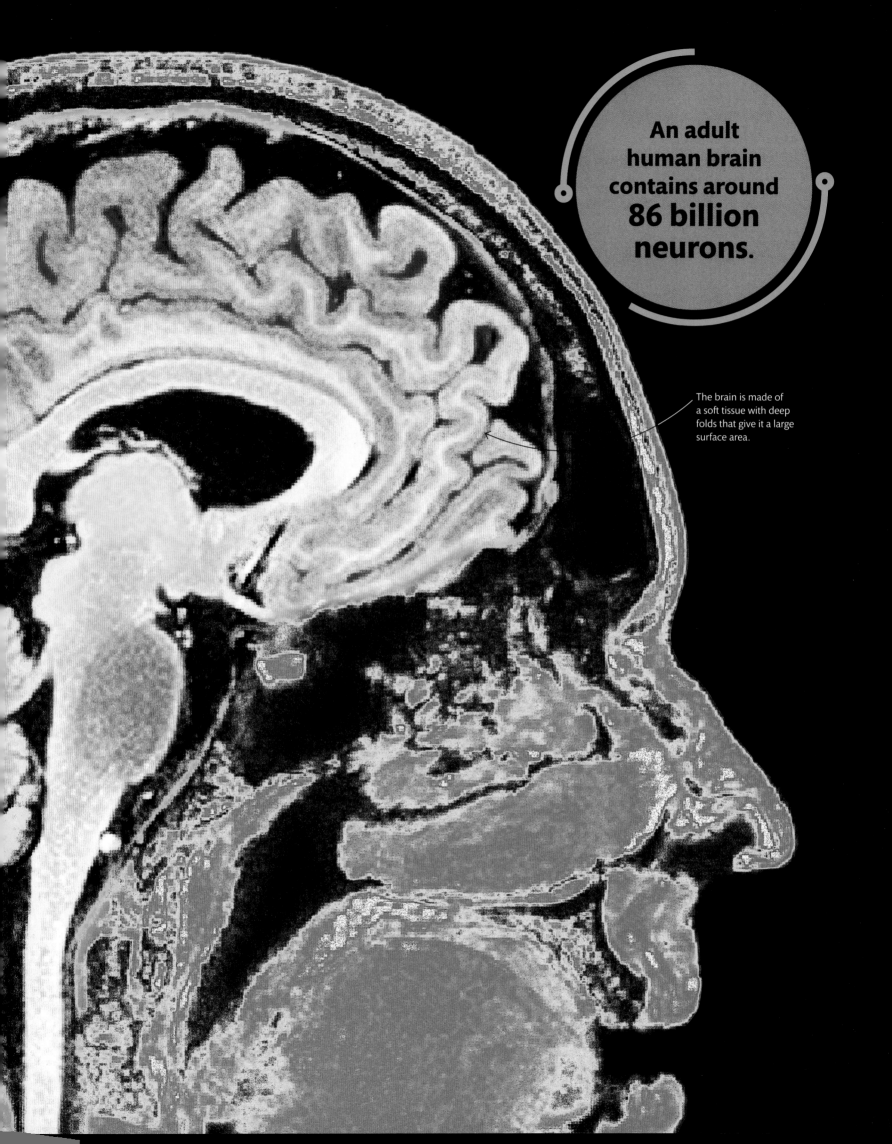

An adult human brain contains around 86 billion neurons.

The brain is made of a soft tissue with deep folds that give it a large surface area.

HEALING WOUNDS

ARTIFICIAL SKIN

Our skin is our largest organ, covering and protecting everything inside our bodies. It is our first line of defense against injury or infections. Small injuries to it can heal easily, but big ones, such as serious burns, are harder to heal. Sometimes healthy skin can be taken from another part of the body and placed on a wound to help it repair itself, but this is difficult to do when the wound is severe. One solution is using artificial skin, which scientists can grow in a lab.

TREATING CUTS

For small wounds, an alternative to a bandage is a hydrocolloid dressing. These are made of substances that swell and form a gel when in contact with a wound. They are flexible and can be used for areas such as elbows, where typical bandages don't stick well.

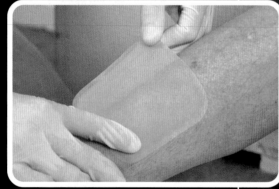

THE SKIN

Our skin protects us from infection and helps regulate our body temperature, and nerves in the skin help us sense our surroundings using touch. Its thin, outermost layer is called the epidermis, and below it is the dermis, which contains blood vessels and nerves. Underneath these is a layer of fat, which acts as an energy store.

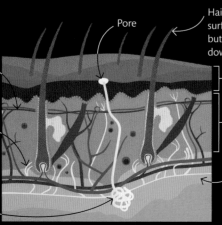

Blood vessels supply oxygen and nutrients to the skin.

Pore

Hairs poke out the surface of the skin but have their roots down in the dermis.

Nerves carry signals to the brain.

Epidermis

Dermis

Sweat glands produce droplets of sweat when the body needs cooling down.

A layer of fat helps keep the body warm.

Skin tissue

The piece of artificial skin below has been grown from cells donated by a patient. The cells are put in a gel, which supplies them with nutrients that allow them to multiply. The strip that forms is made up of a large number of cells and is now described as skin tissue. It can be applied to injuries using stitches or surgical glue.

Artificial skin is light and flexible.

A nutrient gel contains everything the cells need to multiply and form into sheets.

It takes **three weeks** to grow 11 sq ft (1 sq m) of artificial skin in a culture.

Tracking their travels

Common cranes breed in Europe and migrate to northern Africa in the winter. There are many different routes, but among the longest are those from Finland to Ethiopia, where the birds cover distances of more than 4,000 miles (6,500 km). Researchers track their route by attaching a radio transmitter to each bird.

Migrating common cranes can cover around **200 miles (322 km)** in a single day.

ANIMAL TRACKING
MAPPING MIGRATION

Some animal species make long journeys over huge distances every year. This is called migration, and many animals—including birds, fish, and mammals—do it. Animals may migrate when they are looking for food, mates, a safe place to rear their young, or better weather. Learning the routes that they take helps conservation efforts for endangered animals. Scientists can track the animals through a variety of methods, including by using radio transmitters and a technology called GPS

TRACKING SALMON

Sockeye salmon begin their lives in freshwater but migrate to the ocean to feed and grow, returning to freshwater to breed. Like all fish, salmon have bonelike structures in their heads, called otoliths. Their composition changes depending on the fish's age and where it has been. By studying otoliths, scientists can track fish migration

Radio tags run on long-lasting batteries, and some are even solar-powered.

GPS

One of the ways animals are tracked is by using a system called GPS (Global Positioning System). Once a bird is fitted with a GPS tracker, the device sends data about its location to GPS satellites in orbit around Earth. There are about 30 in total. These satellites use the information to pinpoint the bird's precise location.

At least three GPS satellites are used to work out the location.

Satellite signals are sent as radio waves.

Data from the GPS tracker is transmitted to satellites in orbit.

Migration routes

GPS allows scientists to track migrations across the world. Arctic terns have the longest migration of all animals. These birds cover an incredible distance of about 60,000 miles (96,000 km) every year to breed in the Arctic in summer. After this, they fly to the southern polar region to rest and feed in Antarctica.

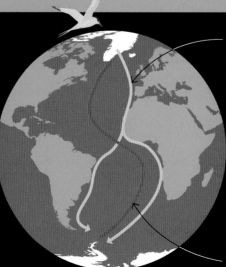

Arctic terns fly south along the coastlines of Africa and South America.

While flying back to the north, the birds take a route that is away from the coastlines.

Eye of the tiger

This rare picture of a tigress with her cub was captured by a camera trap in Bandhavgarh National Park, India. Tigers are elusive and shy, but camera traps allow scientists to study them without disturbing them.

CONSERVATION TOOL

CAMERA TRAPS

It can be difficult to observe wild animals up close so scientists often use camera traps to monitor wildlife remotely. Any animal roaming past a camera trap triggers the device's sensors through either their body heat or movement, which causes the camera to take a picture. These cameras allow conservationists to track wild animals, monitor their numbers, determine their locations, and even study their behaviors. The data collected can be useful in protecting endangered animals.

PLACING TRAPS
Camera traps, such as this one being set up in a national park in the Republic of Congo, must be placed in spots where animals are likely to visit. Scientists have to carefully hide the cameras to protect them from being destroyed by animals or even stolen by people.

CONSERVATION

Despite the efforts of people trying to protect and conserve them, many animal species are in decline due to habitat loss, pollution, poaching, and climate change. The International Union for Conservation of Nature (IUCN) Red List is a tool to examine how likely a species is to go extinct, which helps scientists decide where to focus their conservation efforts. The list has seven categories—from species of least concern to those that are already extinct. Tigers are more threatened than some of their other big cat relatives, but they still have small wild populations.

Tigers are one of the most endangered animals on Earth, with less than 4,000 left in the wild.

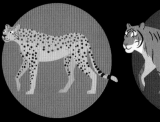
JAGUAR: NEAR THREATENED

SUMATRAN TIGER: CRITICALLY

THYLACINE: EXTINCT

GLOSSARY

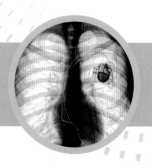

ACCELERATION
An increase or decrease in an object's speed due to a force being applied to it.

ACID
A reactive chemical that has a pH less than 7 (*see* pH). Vinegar and lemon juice are weakly acidic.

AERODYNAMICS
The science of how objects move through the air. The four aerodynamic forces are thrust, drag, lift, and weight.

ALKALI
A reactive chemical that has a pH greater than 7 (*see* pH). Soap and bleach are alkaline.

AIR PRESSURE
The force of air molecules pushing against a surface or container.

ALGAE
Simple, plantlike organisms that live in water and make food using energy from sunlight.

ANTIBODY
A protein (*see* protein) that sticks to microbes such as bacteria, stopping them from being harmful or flagging them for destruction by the body's own white blood cells. When your body encounters a new microbe, it learns to make antibodies, making you immune to it if it enters your body again.

ARTIFICIAL INTELLIGENCE
A technology that enables computers to mimic the human behavior of learning and reasoning. Most artificial intelligence are designed for analyzing data, recognizing patterns, and simulations.

ATMOSPHERE
The layers of gas that surround Earth, held by gravity.

ATOM
A tiny particle of matter. An atom is the smallest part of an element that can exist.

BACTERIA
Microscopic, single-celled organisms with no cell nuclei. Bacteria are the most abundant organisms on Earth.

BATTERY
An energy-storing device that produces an electric current when connected to a circuit.

BIOLOGY
The study of living things. It studies how plants and animals interact with their surroundings. It includes fields of study such as botany, zoology, and microbiology.

BIOME
A region with the same climate, vegetation, and animals. The same biome can be found on different continents. Some of the biomes around the world include tundra, temperate grassland, and tropical forest.

BLOOD VESSEL
Any tube that carries blood through your body. There are three main types of blood vessel: arteries, veins, and capillaries.

BRAIN
The organ inside the head that controls the whole body. This vital part of the body's nervous system allows you to sense, move, think, reason, and understand emotions.

CARBON
A nonmetallic element that is a key component of important chemicals in the body such as proteins and DNA.

CARBON DIOXIDE
A colorless, odorless gas. An increasing amount of this gas in the atmosphere is causing global warming.

CELL
The basic unit from which all living organisms are made.

CHEMICAL
An element, or a substance made of more than one element. A chemical is pure or the same all the way through—it is not a mixture. Water, iron, and oxygen are all chemicals.

CHEMICAL REACTION
A process in which atoms are rearranged to form at least one new substance.

CHEMISTRY
The study of matter and elements, and how elements react when mixed together.

CIRCUIT
A path that electricity flows around. All electrical devices have circuits inside them.

CONDUCTOR
A substance through which heat or electric current flows easily.

CORAL
A simple organism that lives on the seabed in big colonies.

CRYSTAL
A solid substance with a highly-ordered shape. Diamonds and salt grains are crystals.

CURRENT
A flow of a substance. An electric current is a flow of electrons. An ocean current is a flow of water in the ocean, driven by the wind or by differences in water density caused by temperature or salt content.

CYTOPLASM
The jellylike fluid inside a cell membrane, which makes up most of the material inside a cell.

DATA
Information, such as facts and statistics, collected for reference or analysis.

DEFORMATION
A change in an object caused by forces. When an object can't move, the forces can either change the shape of the object or cause it to break.

DENSITY
The mass of a solid, liquid, or gas per unit of volume. A dense material has lots of atoms packed closely together. Less dense objects float in more dense fluids. Wood can float in water, because it is less dense than water.

DNA
Short for "deoxyribonucleic acid," a long, thin, double-helix-shaped molecule found in the cells of all living organisms. It carries genetic code—the instructions for how a living thing will look and function.

DRAG
A force that acts on an object moving through air or water. Drag always acts in the opposite direction to the object's direction of motion.

ECOSYSTEM
A collection of living organisms that share a habitat and are reliant on each other for survival.

ELECTRICITY
Anything related to electric charge. Electric current is the movement of particles with electric charge. Electricity is used to power homes, cars, and many other modern machines.

ELECTROLYSIS
A process that divides substances into simpler parts using electric current.

ELECTROMAGNETIC SPECTRUM
The whole range of different types of electromagnetic radiation, from gamma rays to radio waves. Visible light, which we can see, is part of the electromagnetic spectrum.

ELECTRON
A negatively charged particle found in the outer part of an atom. Moving electrons carry electricity and cause magnetism.

ELEMENT
A substance made of only one kind of atom. There are 118 known elements, about 90 of which occur naturally.

ENERGY
What enables work to be done. Energy exists in many different forms, such as electrical and chemical. It cannot be created or destroyed—only transferred.

EVAPORATION
The process by which atoms or molecules of a liquid turn into a gas.

EVOLUTION
The process by which species gradually change and adapt to a changing environment over very long periods of time.

FAT
An energy-rich substance found in living things. In the body, fats are used to store energy, surround nerves, and as a layer of insulation.

FORCE
A push or a pull that causes an object to change its speed, direction, or shape.

FOSSIL FUEL
A fuel derived from the fossilized remains of living things. Fossil fuels include coal, oil, and gas. They release carbon dioxide and other harmful gases when they are burned, contributing to global warming.

FULCRUM
The pivot or fixed point around which a lever turns.

FUNGUS
A group of microorganisms that feed on plants and animals. They break down dead animals and plants, feeding on the nutrients.

GAS
A state of matter where the particles are spaced out and move around at high speed. Gases flow to fill a container and can be compressed.

GENE
A length of DNA that carries a code to perform a specific job. Genes instruct cells to make proteins that affect one or more of the organism's characteristics. Genes are passed down from one generation to the next.

GENERATOR
A device that produces electrical energy from kinetic energy. Wind turbines and many power plants used generators.

GLOBAL WARMING
A rise in the average temperature of Earth's atmosphere, caused by rising levels of carbon dioxide and other greenhouse gases. Global warming has many effects on Earth's climate, including the melting of ice at the poles, a rise in sea levels, and the occurence of more extreme weather events.

GRAVITY
A force that pulls all things with mass toward each other. On Earth, gravity pulls objects to the ground and gives them weight. The planets of the Solar System are kept in orbit by gravity.

GREENHOUSE GAS
A gas in the atmosphere that traps the Sun's warmth around the planet. Greenhouse gases include carbon dioxide and methane.

HABITAT
The natural home of an animal or plant. It can be as small as an underside of a leaf and as vast as an entire forest.

IMMUNE SYSTEM
The defense mechanism of the human body that protects us from diseases. Every time you sneeze, cough, or get a cold or fever, it is your immune system fighting off a threat.

INFRASTRUCTURE
The basic facilities, such as buildings, roads, and bridges, required by a country or society to work.

INSULATOR
A material through which heat or electricity cannot pass easily.

ISOTOPES
Different versions of an element, each with the same number of protons but different numbers of neutrons in their nuclei.

LASER
(Light amplification by stimulated emission of radiation.) A device that creates a beam of light with waves that are in step and of a precise wavelength.

LENS
A glass or plastic object with curved surfaces that cause light to bend as it passes through. A lens that curves inward is called concave, and a lens that curves outward is called convex. Lenses are used to form images in cameras, telescopes, and microscopes.

LIQUID
A state of matter where the atoms or molecules are closely packed together. The bonds between them are stronger than in gases but weaker than in solids, allowing the particles to move freely. Liquids flow and take the shape of a container and cannot be compressed.

MAGNET
An object that has a magnetic field and attracts or repels other magnetic objects. Things are attracted or repelled by magnets due to an invisible force called magnetism.

MAGNETIC FIELD
The invisible pattern of force that stretches out around a magnet.

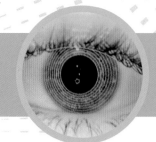

MASS
A measure of the amount of matter in an object.

MATERIAL
A substance out of which things can be made. Every object is made of a material—natural or human-made.

MATTER
The material which everything around us is made from. Anything that has mass and occupies space is matter. Matter includes solids, liquids, and gases, and both living and nonliving things.

METAL
A type of element with specific properties. Metals are usually strong and shiny and are good conductors of electricity and heat. Over three-quarters of all elements are classified as metals.

MICROBE
A tiny organism that can only be seen with the aid of a microscope. Also known as a microorganism.

MICROORGANISM
See microbe

MINERAL
Any naturally occurring substance made up of more than one element that can be found in the ground. Rocks are made of minerals. All minerals are crystals.

MOLD
A type of fungus. It appears on rotten food as a fluffy growth. Most molds feed on decaying plants and animals.

MOLECULE
A group of two or more atoms joined by strong bonds.

MOMENTUM
The measure of an object's motion. Momentum is calculated by multiplying the object's mass by its speed.

MOTOR
A device that uses electricity and magnetism to produce movement.

MUSCLE
Organs in the body made up of tiny fibers. Muscles pull on bones to make the body move.

NERVE
A bundle of nerve fibers and blood vessels that transmits electrical signals to and from the brain or the spinal cord.

NEURON
A nerve cell. Each neuron is connected to many other neurons, creating a network for sending and receiving signals.

NEUTRON
A particle in the nucleus of an atom that has no electric charge. It is located in the nuclei of all atoms except hydrogen.

NUCLEAR FISSION
A process in which large nuclei of atoms break into smaller ones, releasing large amounts of energy.

NUCLEAR FUSION
A process in which small atomic nuclei, such as those of hydrogen atoms, join together to make larger ones, releasing large amounts of energy.

NUCLEUS
The central core of something. An atomic nucleus contains protons and neutrons, while a cell's nucleus contains DNA.

NUTRIENT
A substance that animals and plants take in that is essential for life and growth. Nutrients are useful as a source of energy or as raw material.

ORGAN
A major structure in an organism that has a specific function. Examples include the stomach, the brain, and even the skin.

ORGANISM
Any living thing, such a plant, animal, or fungus.

OXYGEN
A colorless, odorless gas. It is required for a substance to burn.

PARTICLE
A tiny bit of matter. This can refer to atoms and molecules or to subatomic particles such as electrons, protons, and neutrons.

PATHOGEN
A microbe, such as a virus, that causes disease.

PH
A measure of the concentration of charged atoms of hydrogen that determines how acidic or alkaline a substance is. The lower the pH, the more acidic the substance.

PHOTOSYNTHESIS
The process by which plants use the Sun's energy to make food from water and carbon dioxide. This process produces oxygen.

PHYSICS
The study of forces, energy, and matter.

PIGMENT
A chemical that colors an object.

PLASMA
A high-energy gas made of charged particles. Also the liquid part of blood.

POLYMER
A long, chainlike molecule made up of smaller molecules connected together. Polymers can be found in nature, such as DNA, or be produced artificially, such as plastic.

PRESSURE
The force exerted by something pressing or squeezing an area. The same force can produce high pressure or low pressure, depending on the area it acts on.

PROTEIN
A type of complex chemical found in all living things. Proteins are the building blocks of cells. These are made up of simple units called amino acids. There are about 20 natural amino acids, and a protein has hundreds of these units connected in a specific order. Organisms need proteins for growth and repair.

PROTON
A particle with a positive electric charge in the nucleus of an atom.

RADIATION
Waves of energy that travel through space. Radiation includes visible light, heat, X-rays, and radio waves.

RADIOACTIVE
A material that is unstable because the nuclei of its atoms easily break down.

RADIOACTIVITY
The breakdown of atomic nuclei, causing radiation to be released.

RADIO WAVE
A type of electromagnetic radiation that has the longest waves. It travels far and very quickly and can be used to carry information, such as music.

REACTION
A force in response to an opposing force.
See also chemical reaction

REFLECTION
The way light, sound, or other types of energy bounce back from a surface.

RENEWABLE ENERGY
A type of energy that comes from a source will not run out, unlike energy from fossil fuels. Types of renewable energy include wind power, wave power, and solar power.

SALT
A chemical formed when an acid reacts another substance, such as a metal or an alkali. The word is also used to specifically describe sodium chloride.

SATELLITE
An object in space that travels around another in an orbit. Many satellites are human-made.

SENSOR
A device or component of a machine that picks up information from its surrounding environment, such as changes in heat or light levels, and responds accordingly.

SOFTWARE
The programs or set of instructions or data that run on a computer and control how it works, including the operating system and applications.

SOLAR SYSTEM
The Sun and all the bodies held in orbit around it by the Sun's gravity. These bodies include planets, dwarf planets, moons, asteroids, and comets.

SOLID
A state of matter where an element's atoms are joined together in a rigid structure. Solids are firm to the touch and have a definite shape rather than taking on the shape of their containers.

SOLUTE
A substance that dissolves in a solvent to form a solution.

SOLUTION
A mixture in which the molecules of a solute are evenly spread out among the molecules of a solvent. Solutions can be separated in several ways.

SOLVENT
A substance (usually a liquid) in which a solute dissolves to form a solution.

STEAM
Very small but visible water droplets suspended in the air, caused by the condensation of water vapor.

STIMULUS
Something that encourages activity or response in people or things.

STREAMLINED
Smoothly shaped, usually curved, to move easily through air or water.

SUBLIMATION
The process by which a solid turns directly into a gas without first turning into a liquid.

SUGAR
A usually sweet-tasting substance needed by cells to live and grow.

SURFACE TENSION
An effect caused by the strong attraction of water molecules to each other that makes the surface of water behave like a stretched elastic membrane.

SYNTHETIC
A word describing something that is human-made or that does not exist naturally.

TISSUE
A group of similar cells that carry out the same function, such as muscle tissue, which can contract.

TURBINE
A device with rotating fan blades that are driven by the pressure of gases, liquids, or steam. It converts energy into a different form. Turbines powered by the wind or by moving water are often used to generate electricity.

UPTHRUST
The upward force exerted by a liquid or a gas on an object immersed in it.

VACCINATION
Giving a vaccine to cause future immunity or protection against infectious diseases.

VACCINE
A substance given to people to produce immunity against a specific infectious disease.

VOLCANO
An opening in Earth's crust through which magma (liquid rock) erupts, and the resulting structure created by the eruption.

VOLUME
The amount of space an object takes up.

WATER PRESSURE
The amount of pressure exerted by water. The pressure increases with depth because of the weight of water above it. So the deeper you dive in the sea, the higher the pressure gets.

WATER VAPOR
The gas that is produced when molecules of liquid water evaporate.

WEIGHT
The force exerted on matter by gravity. The more mass an object has, the greater its weight.

YEAST
A tiny single-celled fungus that feeds on sugars, producing carbon dioxide gas and alcohol.

Abbreviations used in this book	
/	per—for example, km/h means kilometer per hour
cm	centimeter
°C	degrees Celsius
°F	degrees Fahrenheit
ft	foot
g	gram
in	inch
kg	kilogram
km	kilometer
lb	pound
m	meter
mph	miles per hour
MYA	million years ago
oz	ounce

INDEX

 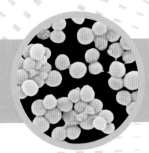  

ACKNOWLEDGMENTS

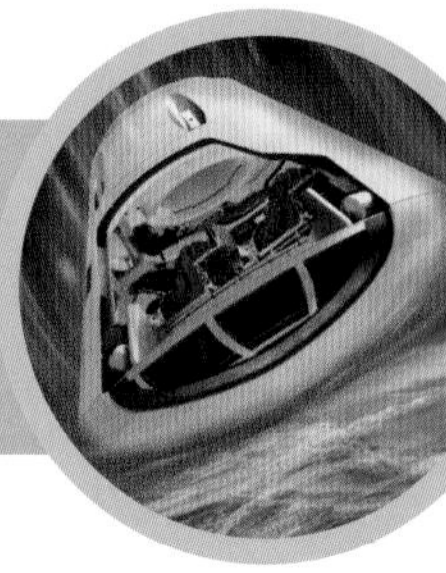

The publisher would like to thank the following people for their help with making the book: Bharti Bedi, Upamanyu Das, Arpita Dasgupta, Priyanka Kharbanda, Sai Prasanna, Bipasha Roy, Anuroop Sanwalia, Shambhavi Thatte, and Vatsal Verma for editorial assistance; Rakesh Kumar, Tanya Mehrotra, Priyanka Sharma, and Saloni Singh for the jacket; and Jo Penning for proofreading and indexing.

Consultants at the Smithsonian Institution:
National Air and Space Museum:
Bob Van der Linden, Curator of Commercial Aircraft, Aeronautics
Matt Shindell, Curator of Planetary Science and Exploration, Space
Michael Neufeld, Curator of Rockets and Missiles, Space

National Museum of Natural History:
Carole Baldwin, Curator of Fishes, Department of Vertebrate Zoology
Benjamin Andrews, Research Geologist, Director Global Volcanism Program Mineral Sciences

Smithsonian Enterprises:
Kealy Gordon, Product Development Manager
Jill Corcoran, Director of Licensed Publishing
Janet Archer, DMM Ecom and D-T-C
Carol LeBlanc, President, SE

Picture Credits
The publisher would like to thank the following for their kind permission to reproduce their photographs:

(Key: a-above; b-below/bottom; c-center; f-far; l-left; r-right; t-top)

1 Getty Images: Pool (c). **2-3 Science Photo Library:** Tony & Daphne Hallas. **4 Getty Images:** Alexis Rosenfeld (ca). **NASA:** NASA / JPL-Caltech (cra). **5 Alamy Stock Photo:** Science Photo Library (cla); Jim West (ca). **6-7 Alamy Stock Photo:** Daryl Mulvihill. **8 Shutterstock.com:** Kimimasa Mayama / Epa-Efe / Shutterstock (bl). **12-13 Getty Images:** The Asahi Shimbun. **12 Getty Images:** Andreas Solaro (cra). **14-15 Octinion**. **14 Alamy Stock Photo:** ZUMA Press, Inc. (c). **16-17 Alamy Stock Photo:** Conrad Elias. **18-19 Cephas Picture Library:** Mick Rock. **18 Alamy Stock Photo:** agefotostock (tl); Jake Lyell (cl); Photology1971 (bl). **19 Alamy Stock Photo:** Farlap (c). **20-21 Getty Images:** Handout. **21 SuperStock:** Biosphoto (c). **22-23 NASA**. **22 NASA:** (c). **24-25 Ciril Jazbec**. **24 Alamy Stock Photo:** OA (cra). **26-27 Peter Trautwein Aqualonis**. **26 Peter Trautwein Aqualonis:** (crb). **28-29 Shutterstock.com:** Ksenia Ragozina. **28 Alamy Stock Photo:** Phil Rees (c). **30-31 Nat Geo Image Collection:** Greg Ludwig. **30 Alamy Stock Photo:** Cavan Images (c). **32-33 Getty Images / iStock:** Chunyip Wong. **32 Shutterstock.com:** Anongnaj Phewngern (cl). **34-35 Shutterstock.com:** urbans. **36-37 Shutterstock.com:** polu_tsvet. **37 Alamy Stock Photo:** H. Mark Weidman Photography (tc). **38-39 Massachusetts Institute of Technology (MIT):** Bob Mumgaard. **40-41 NASA:** NASA / Roscosmos. **40 Alamy Stock Photo:** dpa picture alliance archive (bc). **41 Alamy Stock Photo:** All Canada Photos (bc). **Science Photo Library:** Trevor Clifford Photography (bl). **42-43 Neoen:** (c). **42 Alamy Stock Photo:** Askar Karimullin (c). **44-45 Getty Images:** Loic Venance. **44 Getty Images:** Fred Tanneau (tl). **45 Science Photo Library:** Martin Bond (c). **46-47 Vattenfall Group**. **48-49 Getty Images / iStock:** greenleaf123. **48 Alamy Stock Photo:** Aflo Co. Ltd. (clb). **49 Dreamstime.com:** Bencharat Chanphong (c). **52-53 Boeri Studio:** Vertical Forest Ph. Dimitar Harizanov, Milan, Italy. **52 Studio Roosegaarde:** (cl). **54-55 Alamy Stock Photo:** Ivan Smuk. **55 Alamy Stock Photo:** Dennis Frates (cr). **56-57 BAS:** British Antarctic Survey / Antony Dubber. **58-59 Getty Images:** Ventdusud. **59 Alamy Stock Photo:** Imaginechina Limited (c). **60-61 Getty Images:** VCG. **60 Shutterstock.com:** guruXOX (c). **61 Getty Images:** VCG (tr). **62-63 Getty Images:** Alexis Rosenfeld. **64-65 Alamy Stock Photo:** David Tadevosian. **64 Alamy Stock Photo:** Science Photo Library (c). **66-67 ESO:** ESO / F. Kamphues. **66 Alamy Stock Photo:** Andrey Armyagov (cl); ZUMA Press, Inc. (tl). **Getty Images:** Arctic-Images (bl). **68 Reuters:** Navesh Chitrakar. **Science Photo Library:** Eye Of Science (clb). **69 Alamy Stock Photo:** EyeSee Microstock. **Dreamstime.com:** Martin Kawalski (c). **70-71 Alamy Stock Photo:** Lev Karavanov. **71 Shutterstock.com:** Valokuva24 (tr). **72-73 Getty Images:** Anadolu Agency. **73 Depositphotos Inc.:** Gudkovandrey (c). **74-75 Alamy Stock Photo:** Dino Fracchia. **74 Dreamstime.com:** Rdonar (tl). **76-77 Alamy Stock Photo:** CW Images. **76 Getty Images:** Jan-Otto (c). **77 Alamy Stock Photo:** Reuters (tr). **Dreamstime.com:** Singhsomendra (br). **Getty Images:** Jonas Gratzer (cr). **78-79 Getty Images:** Bloomberg. **78 Getty Images:** Star Tribune via Getty Images (c). **79 Alamy Stock Photo:** Frances Roberts (tl). **Getty Images:** Monty Rakusen (tr). **SuperStock:** Michael Rosenfeld / Maximilian S (tc). **80-81 Getty Images:** Patrick AVENTURIER. **82-83 Action Plus Sports Images:** Imago / Actionplus. **82 Alamy Stock Photo:** Arterra Picture Library (cl). **Getty Images:** George Rose (tl). **Shutterstock.com:** oNabby (bl). **84-85 Dreamstime.com:** Vitalyedush / All. **88-89 Extreme E**. **89 NASA:** (crb). **90-91 Roborace:** Robocar 1.0 (c). **92 Alamy Stock Photo:** riddypix (tr). **94-95 Alamy Stock Photo:** Thom Lang. **94 123RF.com:** foottoo (c). **95 Getty Images:** MarBom (tr). **96-97 Getty Images:** Pool. **97 Getty Images:** Stringer (cr). **Shutterstock.com:** Danny Ecker (br); Konstantin Tronin (tr). **98-99 Alamy Stock Photo:** dpa picture alliance. **98 Science Photo Library:** Dr. Gary Settles (cl). **100-101 Dorling Kindersley: Hum3D.com** (c). **TurboSquid:** 3d_molier International (Astronaut). **101 Alamy Stock Photo:** RGB Ventures / SuperStock (c). **102-103 Getty Images:** Roscosmos Press Office. **102 Alamy Stock Photo:** ITAR-TASS News Agency (tl). **103 Alamy Stock Photo:** Robert Taylor (c). **104-105 NASA:** NASA / JPL-Caltech. **104 NASA:** NASA / JPL-Caltech (cla). **105 Science Photo Library:** Detlev Van Ravenswaay (br). **106-107 Shutterstock.com:** Ashley Cooper / Specialiststock / Splashdown. **108-109 Getty Images:** Christopher Kimmel / Aurora Photos. **110-111 Alamy Stock Photo:** AB Forces News Collection. **111 Alamy Stock Photo:** Jack Sullivan (tr). **112 Bryan Christie Design:** (cl). **112-113 Getty Images:** The Asahi Shimbun. **113 Getty Images:** VCG (tr). **Photo by courtesy of Seatools:** (cr, br). **114-115 Alamy Stock Photo:** Prisma by Dukas Presseagentur GmbH. **115 Dreamstime.com:** Photoeuphoria (c). **116-117 Science Photo Library:** James King-Holmes. **117 Alamy Stock Photo:** Andriy Popov (br). **Getty Images:** Bloomberg (cr). **Science Photo Library:** Mauro Fermariello (tr). **118-119 Getty Images:** Bartosz Siedlik. **119 Alamy Stock Photo:** Aleksey Boldin (c). **122-123 Science Photo Library:** Wim Van Egmond. **122 Getty Images:** BSIP (clb). **124-125 Science Photo Library:** Biophoto Associates. **126 Alamy Stock Photo:** Trevor Smith (cl). **126-127 Alamy Stock Photo:** Science Photo Library. **128-129 Getty Images:** SDI Productions. **128 Alamy Stock Photo:** Science Photo Library (c). **129 Alamy Stock Photo:** Jiri Hubatka (tc). **130-131 Science Photo Library:** Medical Media Images. **130 Getty Images:** Peter Dazeley (c). **132-133 CYBERDYNE: Prof. Sankai University of Tsukuba/ CYBERDYNE Inc.**. **132 Shutterstock.com:** (bl). **134-135 Science Photo Library:** Burger / Phanie. **135 Alamy Stock Photo:** BSIP SA (br); Wavebreak Media Ltd. (tr). **Science Photo Library:** GARO / PHANIE (cr). **137 Getty Images:** Jim Watson (c). **138-139 Getty Images:** Kyodo News. **138 Getty Images:** The Washington Post (crb). **140-141 Getty Images:** Bertrand Guay. **140 Getty Images:** (cra). **142-143 Getty Images:** Boston Globe. **143 Alamy Stock Photo:** Nature Picture Library (tr). **Getty Images / iStock:** Vladimir Vladimirov (cr). **Science Photo Library:** (crb). **144-145 Getty Images:** The AGE. **145 NASA:** (cr). **146-147 NOAA:** Collection of Doug Helton, NOAA / NOS / ORR. **147 Getty Images:** Martin Harvey (cr). **148-149 Getty Images:** Nigel Hicks / Eden Project. **148 Biosphere 2:** The University of Arizona (c). **149 Getty Images:** Franz-Marc Frei / Eden Project (crb). **150-151 Alamy Stock Photo:** Matthew Oldfield Underwater Photography. **150 Dreamstime.com:** Jan Lorenz (tl). **152-153 Alamy Stock Photo:** David Fleetham. **154-155 Science Photo Library:** Tony & Daphne Hallas. **154 Getty Images / iStock:** Georgeclerk (clb). **156-157 Getty Images:** NurPhoto. **156 Alamy Stock Photo:** Reuters (tl). **157 Alamy Stock Photo:** Blickwinkel (c).**160-161 Nick Verola**. **161 Getty Images:** Lev Fedoseyev (clb). **162-163 Caters News Agency:** Geoff Mackley. **163 Alamy Stock Photo:** UPI (c). **164 Alamy Stock Photo:** XM Collection (c). **166-167 NOAA:** ThayerMahan, Inc. Kraken Robotics, and the NOAA Office of Ocean Exploration and Research. **166 Alamy Stock Photo:** Thomas Imo (crb). **168-169 Nat Geo Image Collection:** Carsten Peter. **169 Alamy Stock Photo:** Jim West (cr). **Science Photo Library:** British Antarctic Survey (tr, crb). **170-171 Yuya Makino, IceCube/National Science Foundation.**. **171 Alamy Stock Photo:** Image Source (cra). **172-173 Gran Telescopio Canarias:** Pablo Bonet / Instituto de Astrofísica de Canarias. **173 Alamy Stock Photo:** Imaginechina Limited (bc). **174-175 NASA:** NASA, ESA / Hubble and the Hubble Heritage Team. **176-177 Science Photo Library:** Ikelos Gmbh / Dr. Christopher B. Jackson. **176 123RF.com:** Sergeychayko (tl). **Science Photo Library:** Clouds Hill Imaging Ltd. (bl); IKELOS GMBH / DR. CHRISTOPHER B. JACKSON (cl). **177 Getty Images:** Valery Sharifulin (c). **178-179 Getty Images:** Patrick Aventurier. **180-181 Alamy Stock Photo:** PA Images. **180 Science Photo Library:** Alexander Tsiaras (cl). **182-183 Science Photo Library:** Pascal Goetgheluck. **182 Science Photo Library:** Philippe Plailly (cl). **183 Kennis & Kennis / Alfons and Adrie Kennis:** (br, bc, bl). **184-185 Alamy Stock Photo:** Maximilian Buzun. **184 Dreamstime.com:** Petr Taborsky (c). **185 Alamy Stock Photo:** Ivan Smuk (tc). **Getty Images:** Contributor (crb); Justin Sullivan (cra). **Getty Images / iStock:** undefined undefined (cr). **186-187 John Downer Productions**. **186 Getty Images:** Yamaguchi Haruyoshi (crb). **187 John Downer Productions:** (br). **188-189 Shutterstock.com:** Kimimasa Mayama / Epa-Efe / Shutterstock. **190-191 Getty Images:** Monty Rakusen. **190 Alamy Stock Photo:** Martin Shields (c). **191 Alamy Stock Photo:** Roibu (cr); Science Photo Library (tr, br). **192-193 Science Photo Library:** Du Cane Medical Imaging Ltd. **192 Massachusetts Institute of Technology (MIT):** Rebecca Saxe, Ben Deen, Atsushi Takahashi / Department of Brain and Cognitive Sciences, M (c). **194-195 Science Photo Library:** Klaus Guldbrandsen. **194 Science Photo Library:** Chris Priest (c). **196-197 Alamy Stock Photo:** Mike Lane. **196 naturepl.com:** Ingo Arndt (crb). **198-199 Nat Geo Image Collection:** Steve Winter. **199 Getty Images:** The Washington Post (c). **200 Science Photo Library:** Medical Media Images (tr). **Shutterstock.com:** polu_tsvet (tc). **201 Alamy Stock Photo:** Dino Fracchia (tr). **Getty Images / iStock:** Georgeclerk (tc); greenleaf123 (ftl). **NASA:** (tl). **202 Alamy Stock Photo:** Ivan Smuk (tl). **Getty Images:** VCG (tr). **Science Photo Library:** James King-Holmes (tc). **Shutterstock.com:** Konstantin Tronin (ftl). **203 Alamy Stock Photo:** dpa picture alliance archive (tl). **ESO:** ESO / F. Kamphues (tr). **Getty Images:** Bloomberg (ftl); MarBom (tc). **204 Alamy Stock Photo:** Maximilian Buzun (tr); David Tadevosian (tc). **205 Getty Images:** BSIP (tl). **Getty Images / iStock:** Vladimir Vladimirov (tr). **Science Photo Library:** Burger / Phanie (ftl); Philippe Plailly (tc).

All other images © Dorling Kindersley

For further information see:
www.dkimages.com